The Power of
Doing the Right Thing

The Power of
Doing the Right Thing

Finding Success
Through a Values–Driven Life

James and Terence Elsberry

To order additional copies of this book, contact:
Xlibris Corporation
1-888-795-4274
www.Xlibris.com
Orders@Xlibris.com
34952

CONTENTS

For L.J and Adaline.

ACKNOWLEDGEMENTS

We'd like to thank the many people who have inspired us over the years. We try to tell their stories here and if, by chance, some of the details are amiss, we hope all will know those mistakes are ours alone and that, in the end, we hope to have at least captured the spirit of the individual.

We have to thank our editors, Anne Rice Cumming and Kelly Tracer for their insight, passion and faith for this project as well as our host of other readers. We also thank our wives, Nicki and Nancy, without whose on-going love and support this book would never have been written.

A note about "voice:" To avoid interrupting the flow of a story we haven't bothered to identify which of us is writing a first person account. Usually it simply doesn't matter. When it does, we think you'll find the context will help you identify the magazine editor turned pastor from the newspaper publisher turned professor.

INTRODUCTION

Our purpose in writing this book is to recapture a definition of success. It's the kind of success that will give your life ultimate meaning and fulfillment. We're not talking about material success, although that may be a by-product.

The kind of success we talk about here has its roots in the people we knew as brothers growing up in small-town America. They used a common set of values to create happy, fulfilling lives. We share those values here so you can do the same.

You may read the first story in each chapter and find memories rekindled of other people from other small towns who helped shape your life, people who personify the values we're writing about. Go on to read the entire chapter and compare your life and role models with those you meet there. Finally, you can turn this into a handbook for harnessing the power of a values-driven life for yourself. For that we've included a set of questions for personal reflection and discussion along with suggestions on sources to further your search.

PREFACE

"Life loves to be taken by the lapel and told:
'I'm with you kid. Let's go.'"
Maya Angelou

It wasn't the best hay cutting they'd had that summer, but it would do. He expertly caught the guide rope and swung the last load into the barn. He yanked the release bar and the loose, green alfalfa tumbled past in a torrent of fragrant dust.

He was dark-haired and slightly built but had the corded muscles and over-sized, hardened hands of a man accustomed to hard work. That work had begun as soon as he could pick up potatoes in the rocky fields of the family homestead.

He slid down the ladder and hurried over to the well. He grabbed the pump handle, filled a bucket and then tipped it over his head. The cold took his breath for a moment, but it felt good to flush away the layer of grime. It was time to go in and clean up for his date tonight. He was sixteen and thrilled at the prospect of spending an evening with this new girl.

He didn't know a lot about her. He'd heard she'd lost her parents when she was a baby and was being raised by her grandparents. Like all farm girls, she had to have spent hours in the fields, but you wouldn't know it by looking at her china-doll complexion. She was petite, sprightly and lovely. She was fifteen.

When he went to pick her up he, who was usually so high energy and full of himself, was suddenly shy and feeling a little awkward. She pushed a strand of auburn hair away from her sky blue eyes and flashed him a smile that melted his heart. Later he would say that in that moment, he knew she was the love of his life.

Together in a marriage that lasted sixty-six years, our parents, L.J. and Adaline Elsberry, would meet the challenges of the Great Depression, World War II, business failure and her poor health. Together they would raise us, their sons and would give us financial and educational advantages beyond anything they'd been able to achieve for themselves. Together they'd survive setbacks, heartache and frustration, but they always would have time for others.

Our parents' generation had a saying "You make a living out of what you get; you make a life out of what you give."

Whether it was helping a friend in need, tending to Mother's "little tots" in Bible school or making trips to see the shut-ins they adopted with food and friendship, they were never too busy to extend a helping hand.

They enjoyed a lifetime of hard work, good times, laughter and joy. They fought, shouted and made up. He once said, "I've been in love with the same woman for seventy years, and I've never had a boring day."

Together they would achieve the kind of success that made them role models for their community and succeeding generations. It was a success based on the values of hard work, making good life choices and helping others—a success based on doing the right thing.

And that success started with love. Through all their years together, our parents never stopped loving each other. They spread that love around them—to their children, grandchildren, and a large extended family, to their church, community and an expansive network of friends of all ages.

Seventy years later and not five miles from the site of their first meeting, she lay quietly in a bed at the community hospital. She'd had a light lunch and was sleeping. He sat by the bed just as he had off and on for the past six years. They'd been hard years. Bright, insightful and self-educated, she experienced her worst indignity when her quick intelligence began to fade. Toward the end, she'd sit for hours looking to a distant horizon no one else could see. But one thing hadn't changed. When he took her food tray, there it was again, the smile that still melted his heart.

A few minutes later, amid the drone and beep of the monitors and the soft murmur from the hospital corridors, she slipped away. He sat for a moment, and then reached out to awkwardly pat her cheek. Quietly, all by himself now, he said goodbye.

After she died, the church was filled with people who came to pay their respects not only to a lady of great warmth, charm and character but to a couple whose life together epitomized the values handed down to them by pioneer ancestors, the values that built America, the values that provide the foundation of true success.

CHAPTER I

The Power of Doing the Right Thing

"To get the best out of a man go to what is best in him."
—Daniel Considine

How we define success is based on the people we knew growing up in small-town America. Here you'll read how they built lives on a set of values they summed up in a simple phrase voiced throughout our childhood. In the following pages, you'll read how they set about doing the right thing by using all the values that phrase stood for—old-fashioned concepts such as integrity and perseverance, humility and optimism, faith and hard work.

These values were forged in the heat of struggle and the warm glow of accomplishment. They steered people through both good times and bad and guided them in making crucial life decisions. Our hometown, Clemons, Iowa, wasn't perfect by any means, but its people taught us everything we need to know about how to live.

Here you'll also meet those we've come to know in the years since who have unlocked the secrets of these powerful values and also found success.

This book is not about being perfect. It's about how to survive the misfortunes and tragedies of life without losing your spirit. It's about keeping hope alive. It's about becoming the person your family, friends and the people you work with want and need you to be. It's about you enjoying the power and rewards of a values-driven life.

Success through doing the right thing.

As boys growing up, we saw how doing the right thing brought our parents success. It wasn't the kind of success defined in our culture as having more money, buying more things or having more status or power. Their success was about lives that had meaning for themselves, and for the lives they touched.

You already have what you need to do the right thing. You were born with a moral compass. From your earliest memories, you knew instinctively when you were good and when you were bad. Like so many things in childhood, however, that which once seemed so clear, so black and white, sometimes blurs to shades of grey as you grew older.

Chances are you still consider yourself to be basically a "good" person and chances are you are right. However, doing the right thing is about more than being good.

It's about "doing." It's not about simply thinking good thoughts. It's about actions. It can be as small as helping the young mother with a fussy baby and it can be as large as committing your life to a worthwhile cause.

It works best when you apply it evenly throughout your life. We know. We learned from some of the best, our parents.

When we were young, we took our parents' values for granted. Virtually everyone we knew lived by the same standards. Then, a few years ago we began to realize that the kind of success our parents and their friends enjoyed was based on the values handed down to them. We also saw these values slipping away as all too frequently we saw and heard about people who lived by totally different standards. We realized that in a rapidly changing society such as ours the core values our parents and their world took for granted were fast disappearing.

False gods

Look around you at what's happening in our culture, and you can't help but be concerned. TV reality shows focus on people's failures and shortcomings. So many children have little direction. Parents are lonely. Marriages are failing. Drugs are destroying lives. Consumerism, opportunism, narcissism and greed rule. There is an overall coarsening and vulgarization of our entertainment, in which anything goes and concepts like refinement, dignity and decency no longer have meaning. Anger in America expresses itself in everything from road rage to an increasingly embittered and polarized political electorate.

At the heart of much of this, of course, is a misunderstanding of what satisfies and fulfills us as people. In many ways, our cultural paradigms are bankrupt.

No less than the ancient pagan cultures, many of us have worshipped false gods.

There's the god of prosperity. If the wild spending spree in the first eight years of this century and the global economic crisis it spawned taught us anything it's that the pursuit of wealth for wealth's sake can betray us.

There's the god of information. Historian David McCullough wrote, "Information has become an industry, a god to be packaged, promoted and marketed incessantly. The tools for accessing data grow ever more wondrous and ubiquitous and essential if we're to keep in step, we've come to believe. All hail the Web . . . the Information Highway. We're being sold the idea that information is learning, and we're being sold a bill of goods. Information isn't learning. It isn't common sense . . . Or good judgment. Or imagination. Or a sense of humor. Or courage." [1]

Then there's the god of self. Self-satisfaction, self-fulfillment, self-development, self-potential, self-enhancement, self-sufficiency. Read the newsstands of America if you want to know what, among other things, we worship today. Read how to become a happier, wealthier, better-looking, more powerful self. The ultimate is the magazine called, appropriately, Self.

Add to these the gods of health and fitness, the gods of our hobbies and pastimes, the gods of food and drink, of sports, entertainment and sex and—yes—sometimes even the people we love become gods to us—and you have a panoply contending for our minds and hearts every bit as forcibly as the idols of ancient Rome.

Many of us have worshiped these gods and still felt lonely, frustrated and empty.

More money and more sex and more drugs or alcohol and more effective diets and a more intense exercise program and more buying don't satisfy at the deepest levels of existence.

We need to base our lives on a moral compass that takes into account a much broader view of what makes life worth living. We need to dig up the true gold of values buried too long and make them the building stones of our future.

Living the power of doing the right thing

Between the two of us, we've had careers in newspapers, magazines, freelance writing, education, corporate communications and the ministry. We've lived in eleven states. We've seen firsthand the havoc that doing the wrong thing can bring to people's lives. We've also watched as doing the right thing—as laid out for us by our parents—gave purpose, meaning and fulfillment to people's lives.

You'd be hard-pressed to find more embattled institutions than two we happen to love: the daily newspaper and the church. For years, daily newspapers have been losing revenues and readers. Likewise fewer and fewer people are joining and attending churches. Still, in our personal experience, we've watched two groups of people beat those trends with a values-driven approach to doing the right thing.

The Greeley Tribune

Corporate mission statements have become an inside joke in consulting circles. Cynthia Evans, a former energy company executive, once quipped, "Line up 20 different mission statements and chances are not one person from any of the companies will be able to pick out theirs."

Several years ago, as the publisher of the Greeley (Colorado) Tribune, I watched the staff of that small-town daily sit down to write a different kind of mission statement. Here's what they wrote:

"Do the Right Thing." That was all.

They decided if they made that their moral compass as they dealt with everyday issues, they'd be OK. It sounded simple enough. They knew it was easy to say, but not always easy to do.

Do you run a photo of the fatal traffic accident? Do you publish the name of police officers who kill someone in the line of duty? How about the names of suicide victims? Do you run a series on gang violence even though some advertisers will boycott the paper because of the bad publicity?

In each case, they debated what to do based on what was the right thing, not what was the easiest option or the one that most matched their personal opinion. Sometimes they made a decision despite the fact it could cost a lot of money and even newspaper jobs.

Every department adopted the same approach. Pressmen used the statement to argue about whether to fix a part or replace it. Department heads used it as they wrestled with managing people. Employees used it as they dealt with perturbed customers and each other.

As a result, the Tribune became a workplace based on respect—respect for the customer, respect for each other and respect for and from management and owners.

Before long, the culture became a self-fulfilling prophecy. Talented people who could work almost anywhere came to a small paper in Colorado because they wanted the opportunity to work with other bright people in a friendly, committed, values-driven atmosphere.

The paper won hundreds of state and national awards including those for news coverage, advertising design, fostering international perspectives, support of the First Amendment and community leadership. Three times it was named the best community daily newspaper in America by the National Newspaper Association. It was featured in the Columbia Journalism Review for being one of the few dailies in America to post seven straight years of circulation gains. Although industry sales were plummeting, the Tribune showed continued years of significant revenue gains.

The newspaper also contributed a hefty percentage of its net profits in cash or in-kind donations to philanthropy. It became recognized for its charity work in everything from founding a community emergency fund and a literacy program to seeing that shut-in seniors and migrant families received help and gifts at Christmas.

The staff started groundbreaking new products, including a Spanish-language weekly and an innovative Web site that grew to have as many readers as the print edition.

Perhaps the best recognition came from the employees themselves. In a confidential survey, more than ninety-four percent said they trusted management, believed others in their department and the newspaper did a good job and that they were proud to work for the newspaper.

Despite the perils facing others in the newspaper industry, the Greeley Tribune was a success. How? No one would argue that a bit of luck, talent and a lot of hard work played their parts, but it all began by following a simple premise—doing the right thing.

You can put the same power to work in your own career whether you're the CEO or the newest intern.

Of course, it's easy to see all that get lost when you feel like you're adrift in a sea of "me-first" office politics. Still, those who work hard and are thoughtful and considerate of others never fail to be admired. Sometimes the purely selfish get the promotion, but more often than it goes to the person who is intent on doing the right thing. But more importantly to a happy successful life, they have the admiration and respect of those they work with. You can find power in doing the right thing at work, on the street and even at church.

"All are welcome"

St. Matthew's is a historic Episcopal church nestled on acres of scenic, wooded parkland in affluent Bedford, New York, a one-hour train ride from New York City's Grand Central Station.

For years, St. Matthew's prided itself on being a warm and caring parish. But the generations-old tag line, "All are welcome," affixed to a sign outside the front door, denied another reality. Many people in the surrounding area perceived St. Matthew's not as warm and welcoming, but elitist and closed—the society church of the area.

In 1994, things began to change. Shortly after I arrived as rector, it became obvious the lay leadership was determined to bury the old image. They sought to do this by focusing on two things: They wanted to make St. Matthew's as warm and friendly to visitors as possible, and they wanted to get serious about community outreach.

The unexpected gift of a major bequest put the new vision to a test. Some members said it would be best to invest the money and use the income to run the church. But the majority said the money should be used to help others.

The second group won. They invested the money and began to use the interest as seed money for many life-changing projects. The people of St. Matthew's rebuilt the local community center and rejuvenated the grounds of St. Anne's Church in the South Bronx, a block from the worst drug-trafficking center in the Northeast. They rebuilt two churches destroyed by Hurricane Katrina on the Gulf Coast.

But the church really redefined what it was through the "Raise the Roof" project.

Antioch Baptist Church, a mostly Afro-American church five minutes down the road from St. Matthew's, needed to rebuild and expand its parish house but couldn't raise all the money. Antioch heard about the St. Matthew's community outreach and applied for a grant, which was happily given. But that wasn't nearly enough to pay for the entire project. One of the parishioners at St. Matthew's said, "Let's help them get the rest. Let's help our sister church raise their roof."

And so they did.

These two churches so close in proximity but separated from each other for so long formed a new fellowship and purpose. People who had worshipped within a few miles of each other but had never met began to talk and plan. Together they solicited local businesses and individuals in Bedford and the adjoining towns.

The project culminated with a fundraiser featuring a joint concert by the churches' two choirs. The night of the concert, St. Matthew's was packed. Members of both churches filled the building, but so did other residents of northern Westchester County who'd never set foot in either church. They'd come to support a cause that celebrated unity and the human spirit.

The St. Matthew's choir sang glorious Baroque music. The Antioch choir countered with foot-stomping Gospel. At the end of the concert, the entire congregation stood and joined the choirs singing "This Little Light of Mine." You could feel the roof lift from the sheer joy of people joining together to achieve something important.

While "Raise the Roof" may not have been the largest project the newly invigorated members of St. Mathew's took on, it is one of the most telling.

It proved what they could do when they reached outside themselves to help others with optimism and perseverance. As a by-product, they rejuvenated themselves and their church. Today, the church buzzes with activity. New and old members alike come happily together in community and church projects. The nursery reverberates with the cheerful racket of children, and after services, the parish hall is filled to bursting with what looks and sounds like a joyous family reunion.

The Episcopal Church may be declining nationally, but St. Matthew's is flourishing. Since 1994, individual membership is up seventy-one percent and dollars pledged are up 304 percent.

Why the success? Because people worked together to achieve a shared dream. They've applied to their common life the principles we outline in this book. They care for each other. They help others. They work hard to achieve their goals. They don't talk their faith—they live it.

Now when people read the sign by the front door, they genuinely know "All are welcome."

Doing the right thing is not a guarantee that you or your organization can always beat tough odds and succeed, but it's a good start. A values-driven base is the bedrock for building a team of dedicated people who trust each other and believe in something larger than themselves. Once that kind of team is in place great things can begin to happen.

We can't go back to simpler times, nor would we want to. But the foundations for living that worked then still work today. They can work for you. As we personally wrestled in the mire of life's daily challenges, it was easy for us to miss the gift our parents had given us. In a country that measures success against the winner-take-all of sports play and the annual tally of billionaires' net worth, it's easy not to recognize everyday success when it's sitting on your doorstep. Perhaps, like us, your life will never make a Hollywood screenplay, and there will always be those with more money or fame, but assigning success only to those tiny few is missing the reality of true good fortune. Like you, we've known tragedy, disappointment, grief and loss. Still, taken as a whole, we have been fortunate men.

We're blessed to be in loving marriages. We have wonderful relatives, neighbors and friends. We've enjoyed a variety of challenging, rewarding careers filled with bright, interesting colleagues, and we have a faith that helps us celebrate the good times and carries us through the tough ones.

After a bit of introspection we found that much of our good fortune comes from the love and help from those around us, but for that small part we do get to control, we saw the best things happened when we consciously, and often unconsciously, tried to follow our parents example and do the right thing.

A lifetime of reward

Years after her death, he still paid daily visits to the nursing home where she spent the final months of her life. At ninety-three, he was but an echo of that handsome sixteen-year-old farm boy who first met the love of his life all those years ago. Although stooped by age, he was still energetic and sometimes full of himself. He laughed and flirted with the staff and the residents. His oversized farmer's hands gently helped Eva play bingo and got popcorn for Doris and Bette and Leona. He had been known to carry small boxes of chocolates in his pocket to give to someone who looked like they were having a bad day. He sent flowers to the widows of friends on their wedding anniversary and made a point of sitting and talking with Jack, who was living through the tragedy of a wife with Alzheimer's.

He did all of this until he died in May 2008.

And what did our father get in return for a lifetime of doing the right thing? He built a large extended family of friends who gave him a sense of purpose, love, fulfillment and the courage to make it through tough times.

We hope that by building your own values-driven life someday you can say the same.

Questions for discussion:

- What's a false god in your life?
- What's your definition of success? How will you know when you've reached it?

- Have you been in a situation where someone with power over your life didn't do the right thing? How did it make you feel? What would have happened had they done things differently?

For more on doing the right thing:

- Watch the 1993 movie "Schindler's List" or read the book by Thomas Keneally. What commitments did the protagonist make to do the right thing? What were the outcomes? What did it cost him?
- Read the book "Good to Great" by Jim Collins. See how often business success was built on doing the right thing.

CHAPTER 2

The Power of Perseverance

"As the South proved during the War Between the States,
some battles can be won on guts alone."
—Dolph Tillotson

Eunice Tucker was like a mad wren. She was a tiny woman with sharp bird-like movements and a piercing, staccato voice—particularly when she was on a mission, which was most of the time.

She had married Frank years ago with the hope that he was a rich farmer. He wasn't. Lots of people survived through subsistence farming in those days, and the Tuckers were among them. They had a few acres for row crops, a handful of cattle for cash and beef, chickens for eggs and for the occasional Sunday dinner and, of course, a huge garden. Raising your own food and preparing it for storage in the days before electric tillers and chest freezers amounted to more than full-time work for two people. But the Tuckers got by.

Then to add to the burden, Frank's eyesight began to dim. Eventually, he went blind.

That left little Eunice with a labor-intensive farm, a disabled husband and not much cash. Even though God had given her a body that wasn't cut out for farmwork, he gave her a will that more than compensated.

She worked from before sunrise to past sunset tending to the many things that kept her and Frank clothed and fed. She took in boarders who, for a small bit of cash, got a room and meals. Much she did herself. Brash and unrelenting, she didn't hesitate to ask others to handle the things she couldn't do. Our father and others were called into service to see that the roof got mended and the fence rebuilt—always followed by jars of canned beans or strawberry preserves as payment. She found others to farm the fields for a share of the crop, never failing to negotiate the best possible deal.

But her biggest triumph came from her cakes. Eunice baked angel food cakes in an old iron cook stove powered by corncobs. She'd often rise by 4 a.m. to start the fire. Pick your heavenly metaphor, they all applied to these light, delicious wonders.

No one remembers when she decided to start selling them, but they soon became part of the social landscape. In that part of the county, you simply didn't have a wedding, birthday, anniversary or, for that matter, a funeral without a Eunice Tucker angel food cake. Eunice saw to that.

She created a form of "guerrilla marketing" long before Jay Conrad Levinson's book on the same topic was being quoted in business schools around the globe. Hers was based mostly on the quick, frontal attack. Fixing someone with a Medusa stare after Sunday service, she'd say, "Heard you had a birthday party!" One could see the blood quickly leave the face of the offending party. "Why didn't you have one of my cakes?" Despite the fact that Eunice was at least a head and half shorter, the object of her attention would rapidly diminish in size, shuffle his feet like a seven-year-old bed wetter and promise they'd by golly call her next time.

Subtle? No. Effective? Very.

For all of her work making ends meet, Eunice still found time for her faith and her church. She'd be in the kitchen for the endless string of events and socials. She helped cook and deliver food to shut-ins. And she helped teach Sunday school, where she brought her same head-on approach to teaching the right and wrong of life to one of the few groups that could physically look up to her.

"And the Bible says, 'Thou shalt not steal,'" she'd intone. Same stare, same voice, same effect. After class, we made sure she saw us return every crayon. Sometimes we were rewarded with a brief but brilliant smile that felt like being handed a gold medal.

Eunice never stopped; she never accepted charity, and through hard work and tenacity she made a life for herself and her husband. Many of greater stature and physical strength would have quit, lost the farm and relied on what handouts they could find.

Not Eunice Tucker. She persevered and lived to the age of 98.

Persevering one step at a time

Everyone's been there—the loss of a loved one, an illness, money problems, the overwhelming demands of school, family or work. Life at times seems like too much to handle. "How can I go on?" you ask.

Sometimes the best answer is also the most simple—and the most difficult. Sometimes the only way to continue through life is by consciously deciding to do so. To take the next step. To get up the next morning and go through the day.

As a society, we don't talk much about perseverance, but we have plenty of larger-than-life examples. Lance Armstrong battled testicular cancer and afterward won the Tour de France an unprecedented seven times. Dick and Maurice McDonald failed at making their idea for a drive-in restaurant work outside their home state of California—until they hooked up with Ray Kroc and created the largest food franchise in the world.

Even preschool children know all about "the little train that could."

But some of the best examples of perseverance are played out on a much smaller stage. Call it everyday courage.

Survivors of the Great Depression and World War II taught us that often the toughest but most important thing in living life is finding a way to keep going. While some would be paralyzed with fear, worry, physical ailment or what they felt was the impossible, our role models, our teachers showed us how to get through life. Some did it with teeth-gritting determination and some with a sense of humor. All found ways through tough times by simply never failing to put one step in front of the other.

Some of us expend a lot of energy denying the pain in our lives.

Psychologist Carl Jung once wrote, "Neurosis is always a substitute for legitimate suffering." Often we escape the real thing we fear by focusing on a lesser concern. People can do it for years. Anxieties plague them when what they really need to do is face some basic life fears that keep them bound. When they do that, the lesser anxieties fall away.

But sometimes the problem or pain is so stark, so devastating we can't hide from it. All the escape mechanisms in the world won't help. There it is, squatting in front of us, blocking the path, blotting out the future. Like the old spiritual says, "So high you can't get over it; so low you can't get under it; so wide you can't around it. Gotta go in at the door."

No choice. You have to go through the pain to get to the other side.

Of course some people deal with the serious disease of clinical depression. For them the best answer is to see their family doctor or a professional counselor. For the rest of us, what we need to remember is that being defeated is not a permanent condition. Giving up is what makes it permanent.

Perseverance and the lucky man

Matt Schuman has been a Greeley (Colorado) Tribune sports reporter since he graduated from the University of Northern Colorado in 1991. Matt is an award-winning writer who covers everything from Denver Broncos football to Little League soccer.

Matt works from a wheelchair. He was born with muscular dystrophy, a disease that slowly eats away the muscular system. He needs help to eat and navigate many everyday functions others take for granted. He has limited use of his right arm, the arm he uses to drive his motorized wheelchair and type his stories. By age 35, he had already outlived the mortality tables for those with his disease. With Matt's disabilities, he could easily never leave a bed. Heaven only knows how many times pain and disappointment have knocked Matt down. Still, he's chosen to live life.

I remember days when some angry reader or a downturn in advertising sales had me feeling sorry for myself. About then I'd look out my office window to see Matt wheeling up through the Colorado winter—orange pennant streaming behind his wheelchair, double socks on feet too deformed to wear shoes, Broncos stocking cap and, when one of us would jump to open the front door, the same wide grin. "How's it going Matt?" we'd ask as he motored into the newsroom.

"Great," he'd always say. "Just great, thanks."

I never saw Matt have a bad day, and often his determination and infectious grin erased one of mine.

When his mother died a few years ago, Matt wrote a column about the loss of his only remaining parent, primary care giver and biggest fan. He led with these words, "I'm a lucky man." Lucky, he said, because he'd had such a wonderful, supportive person in his life.

Instead of feeling sorry for himself, every day Matt chooses to live and celebrate life. He chooses to persevere.

Perseverance and failure

Perhaps the first course we should require college freshmen to take should be "Failure 101." We'd teach them life is full of failures, problems and setbacks. We'd tell them, "What you need to learn is how to fail successfully."

There's a recurring story we've been hearing over the past several years in the generation now reaching their late 20s or early 30s. It goes like this, "So-and-so can't figure out what to do. He or she can't decide on a career. They seem rudderless." Just because someone is an adult, doesn't mean they've necessarily discovered their purpose in life. And time and time again, we've seen young people struggling to decide who they want to be when they grow up. It's frustrating, for them and for those who care about them.

But many young people have such high expectations. Sometimes they've gone their entire lives with no significant disappointment. They've passed through a school system that teaches, "Everyone is a winner!" Some have "helicopter parents"—a phenomenon ushered in with the ubiquitous cell phone. These parents continue to hover over their children and manage every difficult aspect of their lives through college and beyond.

These young people are woefully unprepared when real failure—the type that can't be solved by a quick call to Mom or Dad—raises its ugly head. They give up. They lose faith in themselves; they lose faith in their goals. And ironically, instead of learning from failure and striving for true excellence, they become satisfied with mediocrity.

If we fail to teach our young people the meaning of failure and how to handle it, they grow up fearing it. Fear of failure can keep us from taking risks. We all need to learn to fail successfully—to see our failures as inevitable stepping stones to success.

Perseverance and navigating the crossroads

Life stages are normal. But that doesn't mean it's always easy to pass from one stage to another. Often it is not. Jung realized that when he wrote, "Where are the universities to prepare us for all the stages of life?"

Most of our formal education focuses on our early lives. There's plenty of emphasis on babyhood, early childhood development, even the teen years. We lavish attention on the beginning stages. On school and college. On leaving home. On choosing a career, a mate, where to live, what to believe, how to make moral decisions.

But who teaches us about how to be a husband or a wife? Or a parent? Or a friend? Or how to handle a teenager? Much less how to deal with an aging parent or with our own aging? Or the death of a spouse?

Crossroads after crossroads come our way, as time after time we enter a new chapter in our life story. And often we feel adrift in a strange new land, and wantonly unprepared for the current crossroads, whatever it is. It's those times, when all the cards are up in the air, and you know they have to fall, that you feel scared, unprepared and not sure you're up to the new shape your life is about to assume.

You marry the person you love most in the world, and you wake up one day and you realize you haven't just married your beloved; you've married your beloved's family!

You have your first baby, and you're delighted, and it's the greatest joy of your life. But you say to yourself, "Will I ever sleep again? Where is all that time I used to have for myself?"

Your well-behaved, solicitous son is suddenly sullen and uncommunicative. And you think, "Whatever happened to my sweet little boy?"

Or the job, or the relationship, or the robust health you've taken for granted, suddenly is no longer there. Or the children who've lived at home are grown, on their own, and have children of their own. And you still worry about them. But there's nothing you can do to solve their problems.

Or the parent who always has been a loving, concerned, active presence in your life suddenly needs you to be the parent.

Or you face the biggest challenge of all—your own mortality.

Persevering through the toughest battle

Bob Tanner was the primary attorney for Boone Newspapers, a community newspaper company based in Tuscaloosa, Alabama. Tough, funny and buoyant, he became a mentor and role model to many of us as we worked our way up through the ranks of that company.

When you finally got that hard-won promotion, the one that made you feel as though you'd finally arrived, his classic congratulatory note would read: "Congratulations. Now don't screw it up!"

Bob celebrated his ongoing victory over colon cancer with his typical twisted humor by sending an annual e-mail to friends and acquaintances containing a copy of his most recent colonoscopy.

But one year the e-mail didn't come. It didn't take long for the word to spread. The cancer was back. Doctors had given him only a matter of months, maybe a year to live.

I saw Bob at a meeting a few months later. "Elsberry!" he cried across the lobby and charged over with his trademark grin. "How are you?" he asked. And then, before I could answer, "You know I'm dying, right?"

Yes, I said, I'd heard and before I could blurt out how sorry I was he said, "Great, now that we have that covered, let's go get a drink!"

We did so and Bob held court in a corner of the bar with a host of new stories and jokes. That was the last time I saw him.

In his usual bombastic fashion, Bob set people at ease. He took it upon himself to graciously banish the inevitable discomfort we all feel when faced with the mortality of a friend. At the same time, he found a way to persevere for months against one of the toughest battles of all.

Choose to persevere

"But you don't know my story," you may say. "If you knew what I've been through, you wouldn't expect me to keep going like these people have."

You're right. We don't know your story. None of us really knows what another person has to endure. What we do know is that there are people all around us to give us the inspiration to go on. There's always someone who has it worse than we do, yet manages to find a way to persevere.

"But I'm afraid!" you cry. Of course you are. Without fear, there is no courage. Of course Bob Tanner was afraid when he learned he was dying. Of course there have been times when Matt Schuman didn't want to face the pain of living through another day. But both found a way to go on, often just taking one symbolic step at a time.

In fact, the secret to persevering often lies in taking the first step. Psychiatrists advise their patients battling difficult times to split the day into small steps. Get up. Eat breakfast. Dress well. Exercise. Get to work on time. Smile. Do something nice for someone else. Bit by bit, each step is tackled and conquered.

Sometimes each task can seem like climbing a mountain. But taken in small pieces an entire day, a week or a month can go by successfully. And each success will give you the confidence and courage to take on the next challenge. The ability to persevere ultimately reflects an inner attitude of optimism and hope.

Each of us will face our own tough times, times when it seems impossible to keep going. As easy as it sounds and as tough as it may sometimes be, often the way to keep going in difficult times is by simply choosing to do so.

- Who do you know who you admire for persisting in life through hardships that would have made others quit? Consider dropping them a note saying how much they've inspired you.
- What can you take from their example and apply in your own life?

For more about perseverance:

- Read the Pulitzer prize winning novel, "The Color Purple" by Alice Walker. What obstacles did the protagonist, Celie, have to overcome? What was the result of her persistence?
- Do an internet search of Kurt Warner's NFL career. See how many times he persisted after being passed over and counted out to go on to do amazing things.

CHAPTER 3

The Power of Optimism

"I've noticed that most people are about
as happy as they make their minds up to be."
—Abraham Lincoln

Slowly and nervously, we climbed out from under the dining room table to peer through the farmhouse windows. It would have been comical if we weren't all so shaken. We'd run to the usual cover when the tornado had rocked us out of sleep an hour before only to find the cellar full of water. "Under here!" my father had yelled as he pushed us under the heaviest piece of furniture he could find. We lay there terrified while the old house creaked and shuttered in the screaming wind.

Now it was just before sun-up and the world had changed.

The storm may have left the house, but it had taken so much else. The beautiful old barn that we had so lovingly repaired had exploded across several acres of ground. The groves of ancient maple trees were stripped and splintered, their broken bodies lying across the grass like so many discarded toys.

We had lived on the farm for 16 years, and there wasn't a week that we hadn't toiled at improving the place. Now, in a matter of minutes, years of work had been wiped away.

I was starting to fight the nausea and light-headedness of shock when he called me to the front door.

"Let's go to work," he said, "Things are a mess, but we'll get it put back together in no time." He outlined his plan for how we'd begin and handed me a rake as he grabbed the chain saw. I walked to the farmyard and begin pulling the debris into piles. Somehow I felt better.

We know what you're thinking: "Optimism? You mean that Pollyanna thing where the glass is always half full and a positive attitude is the answer to every problem? Get real."

Yes, we want to talk about optimism, and, no, it's not the saccharin variety that's reserved for passé self-help speeches and 1950s television shows. This is a brand of optimism that deals with the realities of life.

Zig Ziglar wrote, "Make every day a great day!" With all due respect to one of the country's leading motivational speakers, that's hogwash. Ride along with a minister as he visits the bedside of a young mother who just discovered she's dying from cancer. Shadow a reporter as he arrives on the scene of a grisly car wreck. Put yourself in the shoes of a couple who learns their new baby has severe birth defects.

Tragedy visits everyone. But optimists know the difference between a truly bad day and one of their own making.

Optimists understand intuitively what Dr. Stephen Covey meant when he wrote, "It's not what people do to us that hurts us. In the most fundamental sense it is our chosen response to what they do to us that hurts us." [1] They know the power of choosing positive responses in life while fully accepting that bad things happen to everyone.

In those truly tough times, the optimists among us will embrace their grief and that of others. They let their emotions flow as they hold their loved ones near. Then they begin the important steps of getting on with life while never, never giving up hope.

Alan Loy McGinnis described a brand of "tough-minded optimism" that sought "realistic, workable ways to face difficulties squarely and at the same time keep an optimistic frame of mind" in his insightful book "The Power of Optimism." [2] As a working counselor, he had compiled a list of characteristics he'd found to be common among those tough-minded optimists. He couldn't have known most of that list described a person very close to us. Following is a discussion on optimism with points borrowed from "The Power of Optimism" and a few examples from the life of L. J. Elsberry among others.

Optimists know there is a great deal of power in accepting troubles head-on and then making a logical plan to deal with them. Those with the ability to "under react" are the people others rely on in crisis. They become the calm in the middle of life's storms others turn to for support and strength.

They also know the best way to deal with problems is to first try to understand the situation and then make a plan to deal with it. But that's only the start. They know the most important part is then actually beginning to do something. Countless good plans and intentions have gone by the wayside for the lack of action. Optimists don't study a problem to death. They begin knowing full well there will be pitfalls and failures along the way, and in so doing, they give purpose and hope to those around them. Often the results can be amazing.

Optimists find a way

Dr. Steve Nicholas knows all about meeting trouble head-on with planning and hard work. His is the remarkable story of a small-town boy from Wyoming who helped eradicate the incidents of HIV-infected babies in Harlem. As a parishioner who became my friend, Steve told me his remarkable story over soul food lunches in a Harlem café. A tall rangy man with sandy hair, round glasses and a perpetual smile, he became serious when he talked about his work.

Steve had a desire to do something that would make a difference, and he toyed with a career in medicine as he studied zoology. "But for a long time, I didn't feel confident enough to think I could take care of another human being," Steve said.

The desire to help proved stronger than his insecurity. He enrolled in the University of Colorado School of Medicine. After graduation, he interned in New York City at Babies Hospital of Columbia Presbyterian Medical Center.

It was 1981, and there was plenty of trouble in the pediatric ward. Central Harlem had the highest incidence rate of mother-to-baby HIV in America. No one knew what caused the disease or how to treat it. People, even medical professionals, reacted to AIDS with uncertainty and fear that sometimes bordered on panic.

Steve wasn't one of them. Instead, he coolly went to work trying to understand the new scourge. When he began, there were no drugs for treating AIDS. Infection was considered a death sentence. One of the first steps in his plan was to find help. He got it from Columbia University, the Samuel and May Rudin Foundation, and the Roman Catholic Archdiocese of New York. An Episcopal layman, he found himself working alongside seven Irish Catholic nuns. They became known as "Dr. Steve and the Seven Sisters."

One of the immediate needs Steve and his team faced was getting infected babies into foster care. They came up with a plan for Incarnation Children's Center, a 24-bed facility that treats homeless AIDS/HIV babies and provides a transition to long-term foster care. Located in a former Catholic convent in Manhattan, ICC has been called the Ellis Island for AIDS babies.

Shortly before the founding of ICC, Princess Diana visited Harlem Hospital. You may remember the tender photo of the beautiful blonde princess holding one of the "untouchable" AIDS babies.

That simple act of compassion spread around the world and opened the floodgates. "The next month, we opened ICC, and the phone rang off the hook with people eager to become foster parents of these children," Steve said.

In its first two years, ICC admitted 170 patients. In 1993, AIDS was the leading cause of death among children in Harlem. Nine years later, due to emerging treatments, the death rate was nearly zero. By 2003, pediatric AIDS deaths in Harlem were rare, and Harlem Hospital had not delivered a single HIV-infected baby. By treating mothers with AIDS, his team reduced the transmission rate of HIV from mother to baby to less than one percent compared to forty percent in untreated women.

His success earned him international recognition. But Steve didn't consider his work finished. "Pediatric AIDS is on the verge of disappearing not just in Harlem but in all industrialized countries," he said. "I could stay in New York and move on to other diseases, but it would be a shame in a world with so much AIDS to turn my back and smugly say I've done my share."

He founded The Columbia University International Family AIDS Program (IFAP), and took his findings to the Dominican Republic, which has the highest rate of AIDS outside of sub-Sahara Africa. He left New York for a year to set up clinics and introduce treatment for HIV-infected pregnant women and a family AIDS program. He hopes to bring answers to other countries around the world.

Over and over, you see practical optimists doing the right thing not because it's fun or easy or an obvious pathway to success. Like Dr. Steve and the Seven Sisters, they do it because they feel there really is no alternative.

Optimists work at enjoying life

It was getting awfully warm in the back of our 1961 Oldsmobile. My brother had his face in another book, and Mom was watching the scenery. We'd left before dawn and now late in the day, I really wanted to be a little grouchy. But I couldn't be; Dad simply wouldn't let me. He was singing, telling silly stories and periodically looking out the window to roar his approval at the Minnesota landscape. "Look at that lake, boys! Have you ever seen anything so beautiful?"

You simply couldn't stay grouchy in the face of his enthusiasm. It was like a seasoning that made anything dished up by life taste better.

Dad liked to travel, particularly when the destination was a ballpark.

He loved baseball. His favorite team was the St. Louis Cardinals. His favorite player was the gentleman superstar Stan Musial. But any professional game would fill the bill.

Somehow a desultory Twins baseball game played in the hothouse of a Minneapolis summer was made special by Dad's play-by-play. "Did you see that fastball son? Must've hit 90 miles an hour!"

Then there were the magic moments such as when Harmon Kilebrew would unleash his giant biceps and knock one over the fence, and Dad would slap my knee until it hurt.

"Isn't this living?" he'd roar.

Then he'd turn to me with a radiant smile and shout, "Aren't you glad you came?"

Thanks to him, I was.

In a society that's become pre-occupied with getting more stuff, it's easy to let the economic engine that fuels our insatiable wants dominate our waking hours. Optimists understand that the most precious things we can give our loved ones and ourselves are times together that turn into treasured memories.

The lesson is simple enough: If you want to enjoy the really important things in life (and we would suggest only some of those happen at work) schedule time to do just that.

Optimists find the positive

Oh, no, he was going to do it again. The sun still wasn't up, but he'd just thumped back the lid on the old upright piano at the foot of the stairs.

"Clang, clang; clang, clang; clang, clang!" He pounded out each of the chords twice then began to sing,

"OOOhhhhhh I wish I was single again!"

It was the only song he knew how to play.

"I wish I was single again!"

I didn't know how he could do it. He looked beat when he came home from work. Things weren't going well. GM was on strike. Like all businessmen, he had bills to pay, but that was tough to do when you couldn't get cars to sell.

"When I was single, I'd make the money jingle . . . ."

Everybody knew he adored Mom. Why did this silliness always make us laugh?

"Oh, I wish I was single again!!" (Clang, clang!)

In spite of ourselves, we all came downstairs chuckling, and there was Dad serving up a hearty breakfast accompanied by his usual grin.

Our father chose not to drag his business troubles home with him. Instead he found a something to make us all laugh.

Let's say you now understand that the only real choice we have in life is how we react. How do you use this knowledge to remove some of the stress in your life? One way is to begin to understand and ultimately control how you think about things. The mental tapes you play to yourself have a great deal to do with how you feel about life. Think of them as personal movies. If you watch a scary movie, you become scared. If you watch a sad movie, you feel sad.

Optimists realize we each get to choose how we feel about life through our thoughts and actions.

Much of your stress comes from worry, and if you think about it, much of that worry is concentrated in things that have happened already or things that may never happen. Either way, it's out of your control. Do you recall past conflicts and play them over and over in your head? Do you recount moments when people were rude, thoughtless or unfair? Do you spend hours playing out what might go wrong in your life? In quiet moments, do you allow yourself to dwell on these things? No wonder you have stress in your life! You have your own built-in stress movieplex!

As a newspaper executive I spent a great deal of time counseling the profession's over achievers when they finally began to crash and burn from the stress in the lives. One wonderful tool we used came in the form of "The Relaxation and Stress Reduction Workbook." In it, the authors write, "It has been well documented that negative and frightening thoughts invariably precede negative and frightening emotions. If the thoughts can be controlled, overall stress levels can be significantly reduced." [4]

They go on to outline how one can use "thought stopping" to begin to control thoughts and emotions. It's a multi-step process but basically involves learning to "listen" to your thoughts and to make yourself stop the bad ones. They even suggest wearing a rubber band around the wrist and snapping yourself smartly twice when recurring bad thoughts pop up. (Think of it as the equivalent of the shock collars some trainers use to capture canine attention when a dog disobeys a command). Then they suggest you replace that negative thought with a positive one.

The wrist snapping technique became so common at the Tribune that Terry Owen, our ever-eager technology manager, even made a game out of this kind of stress busting. When he felt a colleague was over-stressed the stocky ex-marine would stick his boyish, Dennis-The-Menace face in the person's office door, tug the rubber band on his wrist and yell Snap! Snap! While he occasionally would have to duck a flying stapler, he usually was rewarded with a stress-breaking guffaw.

Optimists fill their thoughts remembering good times, planning new projects or doing something positive. As a result, they tend to feel happier and more fulfilled. With a little work, you can, too. Who knows? You might even get up early and make your family a pancake breakfast.

Optimists are cheerful even when they aren't happy

I had stayed after Mom's funeral to make sure Dad was going to be OK. He was tough, but he'd loved her deeply for more than 70 years. Still coming to terms with my own grief, I was plopped in a recliner when he walked past. He was singing. Despite his years, his country-tenor was still clear as a bell, and he was in full voice. Finally, all the tension of the past week welled up inside me and burst.

"Dad! We just buried Mom. How can you be singing?" I said.

He turned to me with welling eyes and a bittersweet smile and said, "Because, son, if I don't sing I'll cry."

Chances are you know people like Eeyore, the sighing, whining, pessimistic toy donkey from the Winnie the Pooh stories. No matter what happens in life, they seem to find sadistic pleasure in pointing out the possible pitfalls and the imperfect. Got a new baby? They'll point out the cases of infant death syndrome. A new promotion? They'll say the company is just looking for more work from you without paying what you're worth. If you come in a room with balloon of happiness, they'll look for the pin.

Then there are the practical optimists. Being around them is like having a personal chef to add greater taste and pleasure to the good things in life. A sunset becomes gorgeous as they exclaim at its beauty. They celebrate the news of a new baby or promotion with such visible joy that each becomes the greatest of blessings.

Optimists address tough times head-on. Like everyone, they can be sad and will certainly sigh and cry. But they seldom do so for long. They instinctively know that the act of finding things to celebrate and smile about, even in crisis, is a gift they can give themselves and those around them. Sometimes the worse the situation, the more we all need something to feel good about.

I was the advertising director at the Natchez (Mississippi) Democrat when the oil industry went bust and we suddenly found ourselves looking at a third round of layoffs in one year just to keep afloat. They were grim times. Unexpectedly, I discovered our father's example of being cheerful when you aren't happy made a lot of sense.

On a whim early one morning, I tap danced into the editor's office, got down on one knee, and with my best vaudeville voice sang "Good morning, Jimmy!" James R. Morgan said something unprintable and threw a ruler at me. Then we both laughed.

Dad was right—laughing helped.

We couldn't laugh at the situation, and we certainly couldn't make fun of those who'd lost their jobs. But we could laugh at ourselves. Sure, we were still upset by the situation. Of course it was often serious and sad, but finding a way to laugh, particularly when we didn't feel like it, was the first step in understanding what it takes to really be a leader. We began to find ways to laugh with our employees. Maybe it was as simple as sharing a joke or as elaborate as doing a silly management skit to kick off a new project. Whatever the vehicle, laughing helped lighten everyone's burden as we found ways to make it through month after month until the tough times finally ended.

The choice is yours

Ultimately, you get to choose what kind of person you'll be and what kind of people you'll associate with.

Here's a test: Ask yourself what kind of person you'd rather (fill in the blank here): "Be married to," "work with," "have as a friend," "promote in your business."

Person A, who overreacts to everything, procrastinates on dealing with tough situations and then bitches and moans and finds fault with everything else—a person who is so very busy with work, worry or life tasks that they never have time for themselves or family and friends.

OR

Person B, who underreacts to problems and will make a plan and take action all while finding things to laugh about and celebrate. A hard-worker on the job, they work just as hard to enjoy time with their loved ones.

There is, of course, no contest. If you'd choose the practical optimist above, then choose to be one yourself.

Questions for discussion:

- Try the "snap-snap" exercise in thought-stopping and see how it works.
- Who are the optimists you've known and what did you like about them?
- Is there a situation in your life in which you overreacted? What was the result?
- How do you take breaks to enjoy life?

For more on optimism:

- Watch the 1995 movie "Apollo 13" for an example of practical tough-minded optimism.
- Read "The Power of Optimism" by Alan Loy McGinnis. Unfortunately it's out of print but can be found in the used section of your book provider.

CHAPTER 4

The Power of Work

"The only place success comes before work is in the
dictionary."
—Vidal Sassoon

I am six years old. The Midwestern sun is setting in a welter of color. I am following my grandfather and his herd of dairy cows as they walk single-file along a time-worn path through rich pastureland to the barn. It's milking time. Morning and evening, cows have to be milked. There's no getting away from the routine when you're a dairy farmer.

Inside the barn, I inhale the sweet scent of fresh hay and straw and grain and old leather. I hear the gentle nickering of horses in stalls next door. The occasional pigeon swoops and coos overhead. Cats stretch and purr in happy anticipation of the milk Granddad will put in a pan for them when he's finished milking.

I hear my grandfather's voice gruffly calling my name. "Get over here," he says. "It's time you learned how to milk a cow."

Milk a cow? I was only six. Grown men milked cows. Milking cows was work. But at least milking cows was easy work. All you did was squeeze and out the milk came.

Or so I'd always thought. To my dismayed surprise, milking wasn't easy at all. I confidently placed my small hands around the brown teats and squeezed. To my embarrassment, nothing happened. Where was the milk? The cow chewed her hay, and I squeezed. Still nothing. I looked up at Granddad, perplexed and red-faced with shame. What was I doing wrong?

"Like this," he said. Granddad took the teats. He showed me that to milk a cow you have to do two things at once: squeeze and pull down hard.

I tried and tried again. Still nothing. I longed to be released, to run and play. But Granddad wouldn't let me go.

"Gotta work harder," he growled.

Bossy munched, seemingly oblivious to the assault on her udder. I squeezed. I tugged. Suddenly twin squirts of milk emerged. I was doing it. I was milking. At some level, I was taking an initial step toward manhood.

"Now you've got it. You're milking. Good boy!"

Delighted with my accomplishment, I continued pulling and tugging, my grandfather grinning approval, until I nearly filled a bucket with the warm, frothy milk.

I'll never forget that moment or my grandfather's pride.

"If you're willing to work, you can do anything," he told me.

Everyone wants to succeed. We want challenging, rewarding careers, happy marriages and families. We want the comfort of material things and the freedom offered by a solid financial future.

Hundreds of books have been written on how to get that kind of success. Attorney Louis Nizer shared the most important secret when he lectured at Yale and Harvard. He told the students he'd give them the word that would make every person a success, a word that would sharpen the dull mind, roll out red carpets and connect them to some of the most beautiful and powerful people in the world. That miracle magic word? W-O-R-K!

Sure, some are born into prestige and power or with an abundance of natural talent. However you have no control over those things.

What you can control is how hard you work at making your own successes in life. If you're going to succeed at anything—a degree program, a career, a marriage, raising children or anything else—you are going to have to work harder than you ever imagined. Anything worth having costs something. And the costs associated with success aren't just financial.

Learning the value of hard work

Our parents' generation saw opportunity at the end of World War II, and by applying the work ethic taught by their parents—they prospered. From 1950 to 1999, the U.S. gross domestic product showed a five-fold growth to create the most robust economy in the world. [1] That economy was built by those who knew how to work.

Some even managed to do so despite tremendous impediments.

I was 13 before I knew Roger Sparks didn't have legs. He was always part of the scene: a deacon in the church, a member of our parents' card party circuit, an active farmer and family man. Sure, he had an unusual rolling gait, but I'd never really thought anything about it. Like others in our community, he was soft-spoken, quiet, self-effacing—the last person who would openly complain about anything.

That's why it was only when a newcomer to church remarked, "Isn't it amazing that he does so much with his handicap?" that I asked my parents what she meant.

They admitted they hadn't intended to keep anything from me—it was just part of who Roger was. Then they told me the story.

Roger had been drafted into the Marines shortly after Pearl Harbor. At the time, the command was desperate for heavy equipment drivers. When they found out he'd spent plenty of time on tractors, they put him at the controls of one of the LCVP landing craft used to drop troops on the beaches.

He was doing that job as part of a flotilla to take one of the heavily defended islands in the South Pacific when a Japanese shell hit the boat. He didn't remember much of what happened next. He vaguely remembered being in the water and later woke up on a hospital ship to discover the strong legs that had carried him over fields and fences were gone.

While others might have spent the rest of their lives awash in regret and self-pity, Roger responded in the way of his generation. He went to work on building a new life. First there was almost a year of recovery as he learned to walk on prosthetics with their artificial knees and ankles. Next he came home and married his childhood sweetheart. Then he bought a farm and began his one-man effort to raise corn and soybeans, cattle and hogs.

Farming back then was often bone-numbing labor, the kind of work that would put many of us city slickers in physical therapy. In the course of a year, Roger would shovel literally tons of feed and muck. He'd slog through blizzards and thunderstorms at all hours to tend his animals. He'd defy the relentless Midwestern sun to make and toss seventy-pound hay bales and stretch wire for fences. Often he'd lose his balance and hit the ground. Always he got back up.

Along with building a successful family farming business, he and his wife had a wide circle of friends and an active social life centered around the church and the school. They had two girls who were as pretty as their mother. Both went on to marry and start their own families.

If Roger had a handicap, it wasn't evident to those who knew him. He built a good life for himself and his family. And he did it with hard work.

Work pays off

It's easy to operate under the misconception that it's possible to achieve great success without working that hard. We see athletes and movie stars who seem to have it all without putting forth much effort. But over the long haul, those who are willing to work the most diligently win. Even mega-millionaires from Andrew Carnegie and John D. Rockefeller to Bill Gates and Donald Trump won their fortunes through hard work and effort. The leaders of America's Fortune 500 companies will tell you the idea of people bringing in millions by making a few deals and then retiring to play golf is largely a myth.

But sometimes those who have achieved success become too comfortable in it. Gary Rust is one man who proved that you can work harder and smarter than even the most successful—and surprise a whole lot of people along the way. I got to know Gary through newspaper circles. Always bright and inquisitive, long after he became known as an expert in our craft, you'd still find him in the front row of seminars while his contemporaries were cooling their heels at the bar.

Gary didn't know a thing about newspapers when he decided to mortgage his house to buy a small weekly newspaper in Cape Girardeau, Missouri. He had worked in his family's home furnishings business, and the odds were stacked against him to succeed in newspapers.

In the 1970s and 80s, the local newspaper was king of the hill. Two thirds of the adults in any community read the paper every day. Newspaper companies made most of their money from advertising, and everyone, it seemed, wanted to advertise.

Many newspaper people equated success with their own skill. They became arrogant and showed it when a new weekly newspaper would appear. "These things weren't produced by real journalists," they'd say to clients over leisurely lunches. "They'll be out of business in a month."

Occasionally one of these papers would last more than a year. But more often than not, the dominant daily in town would buy up the little guy and things would go on as before.

But not always.

This was the case with Gary Rust. The tiny weekly paper he'd bought was failing miserably in a fight with the hometown daily, which was owned by one of the largest newspaper companies in America.

"My father came out of the Depression," Gary told me. "He never finished high school, but he knew how to work. Work was expected of us, we worked hard, and we did it well."

Gary applied that same philosophy to his new business. His reporters logged long hours to fill the paper with local news while the daily stuffed page after page with national wire stories. He began publishing the paper three times a week and spent countless hours with advertisers.

"Being a retailer myself helped," he said. "I knew how they thought. I'd give them the best advice I could, including not buying my product if I thought that was the right thing. The publishers at the daily never spent much time with clients."

He offered better advertising rates and, eventually, better results. Then he plowed his profits back into building a better product. What he didn't know, he learned. He read, studied others and attended every industry training session he could.

He and his people captured the hearts and minds of their readers and the pocketbooks of advertisers. The daily paper had many more employees, the support of a multimillion dollar corporation and more than 100 years of owning the market.

After ten years of battle, turning over three different publishers and repeated attempts to buy Gary's paper, the huge media conglomerate did the unthinkable. They sold out to the upstart. The Southeast Missourian was Gary's first daily newspaper.

That was decades ago. Gary has since turned the company over to his two sons. Today, Rust Communications owns and operates 40 newspapers in 14 states. You can still hear the pleasure in his voice when he recalls how they got started.

"In retail, I learned you have to sometimes work six or seven days a week. The other guys were never willing to do that," he said. "It was a hard-nosed struggle, but the hard work paid off."

Work and the entitlement epidemic

One of the potential roadblocks to using the power of work in our own life is what some have dubbed the "entitlement epidemic." You can trace the financial crisis of 2008-2010 in part to this cultural disease. People moved into bigger homes, bought more expensive cars and filled their garages with everything from Harleys to speedboats, many using credit, and not real wealth, to do it. Many in our culture have come to expect these things as necessities, not luxuries. Several generations have grown up believing they are entitled to them—with little or no effort on their part.

Psychologist David Walsh, author of "No: Why Kids of All Ages Need to Hear It and Ways Parents Can Say It," coined the phrase "discipline deficit disorder" to refer to the condition of people who become impatient when their inflated expectations in life aren't met.[2]

Some blame this lack of discipline on permissive parents, schools that insist all children are brilliant regardless of achievement level, soccer leagues that give out trophies just for showing up or the over-the-top materialism promoted by the thousands of advertising images that bombard us daily.

More and more people, it seems, not only want every material possession the good life can offer, they seem to think it's their right to have those things. They have an elevated sense of their own importance, and if they don't get immediate gratification, they may pout and whine.

Courage, vision and hard work

There are still plenty of people who don't suffer from an entitlement epidemic. Instead, they inspire others with their vision and willingness to do what it takes to succeed. One of them is Whitney Johnson. I watched Whitney grow up—her parents had always been active in the church so the bright, happy child with the ready smile was something of a fixture in the parish, but nothing had prepared me for the depth of her compassion.

Her idea of success was transformed after she spent a semester abroad in Cape Town, South Africa.

The 26-year-old grew up in New York and attended Colorado College. During her time in Cape Town, she volunteered in a home for children orphaned by the AIDS epidemic. Whitney fell in love with the children. Her six-month sojourn turned into a year. She came back to the U.S. and got her degree.

Many people who travel abroad come home with their eyes opened to the needs of the rest of the world. But for most, the experience fades after a few weeks of settling back into their routine.

But Whitney couldn't get the children out of her mind. She had more than a desire to do something—she had courage, vision and the work ethic to turn her new-found passion into something meaningful.

Within two years of graduation, Whitney formed an organization, Ubuntu Africa, dedicated to providing health care and support services for HIV positive children in South Africa. Ubuntu means "I am because we are." It's an African phrase that means we are all connected. Under Whitney's direction, Ubuntu Africa has opened a children's health care center in Khayelitsha, the largest township outside of Cape Town and one of the most impoverished in South Africa.

The children who attend Ubuntu's health care center range in age from four to eighteen. Nearly all have contracted HIV from their mothers at birth or through sexual abuse.

While the ready smile of her childhood is never far away, her face now alternately reflects the determination of hard work and heart-felt empathy as she talks about her life's work. "Disturbing doesn't come close to describing the faint and silent presence of a child who has never known love or joy," Whitney said to me. "When a child can't make eye contact, I always have the same feeling. It's the sense that this child has no idea of the worth of their own presence, of how loveable and beautiful they truly are. These children don't meet another's eyes, because in order to seek that love and connection, they must first know that it exists."

We don't often link love with hard work, but that's exactly what Whitney and her colleagues do every day as they work long hours not only taking care of the children but also showing them that they are loved.

"Many children with HIV have to face illness alone, and it's true that the prognosis for them is very poor. But the children at our center know love and joy. Because of that, I believe their prognosis is different," she said.

Because of Whitney's dedication and hard work, these forgotten children are given the twin life lines of love and hope.

When you can work too much

Most people understand the difference between working hard and being a workaholic. Hard work is often the key to success in life, but spending all your waking hours on work is a formula for personal disaster. In his book, "Chained to the Desk," Bryan E. Robinson points out that more people are taking less time for family, friends and simple activities such as family vacations.

He writes that there's a difference between those who work hard and the workaholic. "Healthy workers know when to close the briefcase, mentally switch gears, and be fully present at a son's Little League game or the celebration of their own wedding anniversary. Workaholics allow work to engulf all other quarters of life . . . commitments to self-care, spiritual life, household chores, friends, partners and children are frequently broken to meet work deadlines."[3]

It's important to not fall into the workaholic trap. A life spent always at work is not a life, and regardless of the rewards it may bring, it can hardly be called a successful one.

I understand this sort of thing better than I'd like. For me, more than thirty years of hard work and success were inexorably linked. At the Greeley Tribune, success came by working as hard as needed to buck declining industry trends in readers and advertising revenue. For years, sixty-plus hour work weeks were the norm for the entire management team. Eventually even that wasn't enough.

From August through December 2006 I worked all but five days, two of them holidays. I raced from client calls and civic responsibilities to project planning meetings and budget sessions and choked down too many hasty lunches and dinners at my desk.

By mid-December, the adrenaline rush that had carried me for years was beginning to take its toll. I have a heart condition called atrial fibrillation. It means the upper chamber of the heart, the atrium, will begin to beat rapidly all by itself. It's fairly common and, in small doses in healthy younger people, not all that dangerous. Mine was spinning out of control. I was going into a-fib for as much as 14 hours at a time, often day after day. Imagine having your heart race at up to 180 beats a minute for half a day. At best, it's draining. I remember coming home late at night and trudging up the stairs, each foot feeling as if it weighed fifty pounds.

While the physical effects of my work schedule were becoming obvious, the mental and emotional effects were more hidden—at least to me.

I was home early for a Friday night and my wife asked me to accompany her to a charity event. She was miffed when I declined and said so.

I snapped and yelled something unprintable. The dam burst for her as well. She told me she was tired of watching me destroy our relationship and myself. She reminded me that people with my heart condition had a 500 percent increase in the chances of having a stroke. Then she paused, and her brown eyes filled with tears. "Why are you doing this?" she whispered.

I had no ready answer. Together we'd made decent money and had been smart with it. That meant we could get by without my salary. Certainly no one was making me work so hard. The stockholders and president of the company always had been supportive and gracious.

The conversation that began that night continued for months. My wife and I enlisted the aid of my physician, a professional counselor and close friends. Still, I was in denial. I took pride in being the fixer of problems, the leader and motivator. I cherished my work relationships. I wasn't about to let it all go.

Eventually my support team convinced me that, for me, continuing to work at a newspaper was like an alcoholic tending bar. I was hard-wired to work as much as needed to succeed. Given the ongoing challenges facing the industry, I would always find reasons to spend increasingly long hours on the job.

So I said goodbye to a thirty-two-year career that had been filled with challenge, opportunity and rewards. Unfortunately, it was a career built on a business that easily fostered workaholics, and I had become the poster child.

Since then, I've taught classes at the local university, worked in our yard and garden, cooked many meals for my wife and our friends and exercised regularly. As a couple, we've visited family, traveled, hiked and fly fished in the nearby mountains and have spent long evenings together.

My health-threatening a-fib is almost completely gone.

I have a new career, and it's based on working hard not just at work but life and love as well. And this time you could say my heart is in it.

Maybe you're the kind of person who needs work like others need their fix of booze or cocaine. If you are, we suggest you get professional help. For the rest of us, it's important to follow the example of our hard-working father who loved family vacations, singing in the church choir and parties with friends.

How to work at redefining success

Real success carries a much broader definition than material gain. To feel truly successful in life, consider committing to and working hard at any of the following:

- Being the sort of person others can depend on.
- Raising a child.
- Building a marriage based on empathy, love and mutual respect.

- Caring for an elderly parent.
- Taking an active role in making your community a better place.
- Volunteering for a charity to help those less fortunate than yourself.
- Becoming active in the political process.
- Befriending and mentoring a young person who's not your child.
- Being the kind of friend others can turn to in tough times.

The rewards can be wonderful. Our grandfather was never a rich man, but all his years of hard work paid off with the great joy of spending the last twenty years of his life on the family farm, where almost every Sunday he reveled in the company of his children and grandchildren. Who knows what desperate moments Roger Sparks experienced as he began to build a life after his horrible injury? Despite that he built a good life for himself and his family. Gary Rust may have more money than he ever imagined, but he'll tell you the real joy comes in providing good jobs and serving communities. Whitney Johnson may not be pursuing the same kind of success others in their twenties are going after, but she'll tell you her sense of accomplishment comes in seeing the changed lives of South African children.

First make an effort to understand what's really important in your life. Then work as hard as you can to make it happen. When you do, you'll discover what Louis Nizer was talking about. Work really is the magic word.

Questions for discussion:

- Do you know someone who has succeeded more by hard work than natural talent?

- Columnist James Thurber wrote, "The harder I work, the luckier I get." What do you think he meant?
- Do some Internet research about how many hours a week various professionals work. Are you surprised by the answers? (Look at doctors, lawyers, business owners, etc.)

For more on work:

- Watch the movie "The Pursuit of Happyness." What does the film mean to you?

CHAPTER 5

The Power of Affirmation

"There is no exercise better for the heart than reaching
down and lifting people up."
—John Holmes

Garnet Griffiths always could find a four-leaf clover, whether it was hidden in a lush Iowa lawn or tucked away in the heart of a child.

She was a beautiful woman, but that's not why we remember her. Tall, statuesque, she held herself like a queen. A nimbus of silvery hair crowned her lovely blue-eyed, wide-browed face. An Iowa farmer's wife, she wore sophisticated city suits to church that made other women look frumpy by comparison.

But the children fortunate enough to have Garnet as a Sunday school teacher loved her not because she was beautiful. We loved her because being with her made us feel good about ourselves.

Garnet had the gift of affirmation. She called forth the best in people, wonderful talents we didn't know we possessed until she showed them to us. She'd find the best in a child, no matter how deeply it was hidden, and then her praise would burnish it to a high sheen. Class after class of children became like strings of Christmas tree lights she plugged in so that for a few minutes on Sunday mornings we each shone with our individual brilliance.

In her presence, dull children sparkled. The tongue-tied among us found eloquence. Homely girls, lit by Garnet, became pretty. Ornery boys turned into little gentlemen.

Garnet didn't just value us—she treasured us. She made you feel important. We never heard her say a negative or an unkind word. Everything she said was positive. And she had profound wisdom.

"Everyone has a talent," she would say. "God has given each of us a gift. We are hand-made by Him to use our gift so we can carry out the purpose He has in mind for us. Find your purpose, and you'll find happiness."

No child was too young or too awkward or too difficult for Garnet to begin the happy task of not only finding our special talents, but also helping us determine our purpose in life. An uncanny insight accompanied her affirming ways.

Garnet had another gift that was a metaphor for her abilities with children. She often visited our home, and in summer, I would follow her out to her car and beg her to do what nobody but Garnet could do. Acquiescing, she'd look over the farmyard's rich mosaic of grasses and native plants. After a moment, she'd bend down and pluck a four-leaf clover. I could spend endless amounts of time fruitlessly trying to find one. Garnet always did it at once.

She did the same with children. She could look at the rough slate of a child's personality and uncannily determine what we should do when we grew up.

One day Garnet said, "Terry, you should go into the ministry. I know it's right for you."

I didn't tell Garnet, but the last thing I wanted to be when I grew up was a minister. I wanted to be rich and famous, not preaching sermons and spending my time with sick people. I remember thinking, "Garnet may get it right a lot of the time, but she's wrong this time. I'll never be a minister."

Time passed. I grew up, married, had children and worked through a series of careers—none of them the ministry.

Then at age thirty-eight, I was called to be an Episcopal priest. I hadn't talked with Garnet for a long time when I began my studies at Virginia Theological Seminary in Alexandria, Virginia. Then my father told me she was dying of cancer. I wrote a letter thanking her for all she'd done for me and so many others. I told her she'd been right after all, that I was the happiest and the most fulfilled I'd ever been. I told her I would always be grateful to her for affirming my calling so many years before I knew it existed. It may have taken more than 25 years, but I'd finally found Garnet's four-leaf clover.

Think of your life as a play. If you're fortunate, you have some "balcony people." Balcony people are the ones who, no matter how the performance is going, are always there in the balcony cheering you on. They'll give encouragement when you fall on your face and will be the first with a standing ovation when you're spectacular.

The power of their affirmation can carry you through the toughest times and make you reach for achievements you never thought possible. We were lucky growing up. We had a whole village of balcony people like Garnet Griffiths.

Having someone believe in you even more than you believe in yourself can be a powerful thing. It can help people stretch to heights they didn't think possible. It worked in Garnet's Sunday school class, it works in business, and it can certainly work for you. Unfortunately, you have little control over how many balcony people you have in your life, but you can put the power of affirmation to work for yourself as a leader, spouse, parent or friend.

Affirmation works in the workplace

James B. Boone, Jr. is not a demonstrative man. With his white, thinning hair, Winston Churchill frame, Ivy League blazers and ties, one could mistake him for an accountant or college professor. But his eyes tell a different story. They can go from glinting, gun-metal grey when he's challenged to merry slits when he releases an infrequent chuckle. When those eyes are turned on you as he listens to what you have to say, they can brighten your world.

Boone is the chairman of the board of Boone Newspapers Inc.—a company he built from the ground up. Today it includes more than 40 newspapers. At age 29, I had the good fortune to have an office two doors down from Mr. Boone. As a junior member of his management team, I got to watch first hand as he built his company with a daring formula: Find broken down, poorly-run newspapers few others would want and then be willing to pay more than anyone else to acquire them. Despite often being highly leveraged with his creditors in the early years, he always found a way to make the newspapers not only profitable, but often very good at their craft. His papers have won hundreds of awards for excellence. He's never defaulted on a loan payment, and his word is widely recognized to be as good as an iron-clad contract.

He has a penchant for detail that any engineer or accountant would envy, and despite his restrained, buttoned-downed personality, he has the power of affirmation.

For years, he was a very active owner. He often visited his newspapers and didn't just talk with management. He'd greet the receptionist and ask about her son's graduation. He'd call a pressman by name and ask if he'd solved the problem with the number three unit. He'd stop an advertising salesperson and ask her how last week's major account presentation had gone.

Then, in each case, he would do the most amazing thing: He would listen. He would listen by focusing those brilliant eyes on the speaker and blocking out all else. For those few minutes, each person felt like the most important employee in the company. They knew his interest was genuine, his comments and compliments honest and sincere. This man of great dignity dignified them as he listened with courtesy, intelligence and respect.

Further, his employees knew he rewarded talent wherever it lay regardless of the package it came in. Long before it was popular, age, race, gender and background counted little in the Boone organization. What did count was work ethic, integrity and ability. In a deep South that had been racked with racial politics and boycotts, he made a bright, young black pressman the production director of his largest printing plant. A middle-aged woman with a high school GED became his most successful advertising director. A recovered alcoholic was promoted to publisher. A young man in his twenties was made company president.

He saw their latent talent and potential, and each blossomed under the responsibilities he gave them.

The Boone organization became known for having some of the best and brightest in the industry. What most didn't know is that many of his employees became the best and brightest because of the affirmation given by a remarkable man.

Though very different, Jim Boone's sparse, focused approach and Garnet Griffith's loving, intuitive style teach us to do the following to make the power of affirmation work in our lives.

Affirm by listening

There is no better way to show your interest in others. Management coaches tell their clients to use "active" listening skills: lean in and look into the speaker's eyes. Nod. Ask questions. Use verbal cues to urge them on such as "Really!", "No kidding," even a simple "Uh-huh." All telegraph that you're not only interested in what the speaker has to say but that you value them as a person. These small actions can work wonders.

The wildly charismatic Wallis Simpson, the twice-divorced American whose relationship with King Edward VIII prompted him to abdicate the British throne, apparently understood this skill. The story goes that Winston Churchill once had dinner with the socialite Lady Thelma Furness and Wallis, then the Duchess of Windsor, on successive nights. About the two women he's reputed to have said, "When with Lady Furness, you felt she was the most fascinating person on earth. When with the Duchess, you felt you were the most fascinating person on earth."

Affirmation avoids the perfectionist's trap

Few things in life are perfect, and if you only wait for those moments to give affirmation to yourself or those around you, you'll be missing out on a lot of affirmation opportunities. People instinctively know when they deserve praise, and criticism at those times can have devastating effects.

We have a friend who still bears the scars of being raised by a perfectionist mother. He's a brilliant businessman who has successfully served as president of two different companies. Though recognized as an innovator and leader in his field he still regresses to an unhappy teenager when he talks about his childhood.

He says, "I remember coming home with my report card. I was bursting with pride. Not only did I have straight A's but I had actually received the first grade higher than a B+ ever given by a demanding chemistry teacher." To this day, a shadow falls over his face as he continues: "I anxiously handed the card to my mother, and she studied it for a few moments. After a long pause the only thing she had to say was, 'What's this A-minus in chemistry?'"

Nitpicking the imperfect while overlooking the good is hurtful in any kind of relationship. Still, it can be easy to fall into, especially when dealing with family and co-workers.

Affirmation doesn't starve the whales

Here's a story we used in training new managers on how to not fall into the perfectionist's trap.

A man visits Sea World for the first time. He has a great day but is most impressed by the Killer Whale exhibit. He's transfixed by the amazing feats performed by the massive stars of the show. The climax comes when the trainer climbs a thirty-foot tower and holds two basketballs over the water. Two whales race around the tank then go airborne like NBA stars only to delicately take the balls from the trainer's hands before splashing down to the crowd's delight.

Afterward, the man goes up to the trainer.

"That was simply wonderful," the man said.

"Thanks," said the trainer. "They're remarkable animals, aren't they?"

"They sure are! But I have one question," said the man. "How did you ever train them to perform that last trick?"

"Well," said the trainer, "it takes a long time. First we give them a fish when they come near the balls, then we gradually begin to move them to the edge of the tank and then higher and higher into the air. Each time they touch the balls we give them a fish. All in all, it takes about a year to get them to jump like that."

"Wow! That's a long time. Why didn't you just refuse to feed them unless they jumped 30 feet into the air and got the balls?" asked the man.

"We tried that," said the trainer, "but we starved a lot of whales."

You simply can't wait until someone does something perfectly before giving praise. If you do, they may never even make the attempt. Often it's important to reward their first steps taken in the right direction. Don't be stingy with praise.

Scientifically, affirmation can be viewed as simple behavior modification. Give progressive rewards for behavior as it goes in the right direction and you can get most creatures to do amazing things. With patience and some kernels of corn you can get pigeons to walk tight ropes. Use the same approach and large chunks of meat and lions can be trained to jump through flaming hoops.

Animals will modify their actions for food. Our love of the free lunch not withstanding, humans usually need something that appeals on a different level. One of the most powerful of these motivators is an honest compliment.

Affirm by catching people doing the right thing

Affirmation begins to cast its spell when we recognize others as they start to do the right thing. The key is to catch people doing something right and reward them. The lazy teen who takes out the trash without being told, the grumpy co-worker who stays a little late to help you finish a project, the forgetful spouse who remembers an anniversary—all deserve a heart-felt thanks. That small reward pushes them closer to repeating good behavior in the future.

Several years ago, the Greeley Tribune management team created "Caught in the Act" cards to reward staffers for doing the right thing. The size of a business card, they could be passed out by any manager at any time when they caught an employee in the act of working above and beyond the call of duty. Cards could be accumulated and turned in to the HR department for company merchandise such as baseball caps or sport shirts. The hardworking employee who got more than twenty cards in a year could turn them in for a $100 bonus.

Usually the recipient had given exceptional service to a customer. Maybe they pulled a double shift to get out a major story or suggested a more efficient way to process bundles of papers. Receiving a card served as proof that someone had noticed and appreciated hard work well done.

The cards became wildly popular with both staff and management. "Card that person!" became a phrase used by everyone in the organization to point out someone who had done something exceptional.

People loved the "Caught in the Act" cards not just for the prizes they awarded, but because they helped create a culture where good work was recognized and rewarded.

Affirmation and telling the truth

The people who worked for Jim Boone knew one of his compliments was a prize worth receiving because it was based on honesty. As a result, each bit of praise made them want to work that much harder. You know when you've done something well. Doesn't it feel good when someone else notices and tells you so? On the other hand, how do you feel when you get effusive praise for doing very little? It feels cheap and false, doesn't it? Remember that when you give compliments. Avoid overkill and exaggeration when a simple, sincere, statement such as, "Gosh, that was well done. Thank you," will do. Said in the right place, at the right time and in the right way, it can be powerful.

Sometimes, the person giving the praise can see truths you can't. Certainly Garnet Griffiths saw the truth of our potential long before we did, and, in her loving, supportive way, she challenged us to live up to that vision.

Affirm through challenge

As assistant to the Reverend Jack Bishop I saw how he affirmed others by challenging them to be the best they could be. Jack was a short, bald, fit ex-marine with a blazing smile. As the rector of a large, affluent Episcopal church in Greenwich, Connecticut, he had his pick of both clergy and lay people when filling staff positions. Regardless of their skill level, however, nearly everyone who ever worked with Jack said he found ways to push them into doing things they didn't think they were capable of. "I think of myself as merely lifting off manhole covers," he said. "When you walk down the street and see steam rising through a manhole cover you know there's a lot of energy down there. Someone just needs to lift it up to let the energy out. All I do is help people release the talent they already have."

Affirmation isn't just about giving compliments. Often it's about challenging people to exceed their own expectations. Think of your favorite teacher, coach or boss. Chances are they challenged you more than anyone else. They pushed you to do things you didn't think possible, and when you eventually did them, they congratulated you for your victory. He or she may have been a stern disciplinarian or a warm, cheerleader type. Either way, they became your favorite because you realized they helped you reach new heights by believing in your potential even more than you did.

Affirm when others need it most

Sometimes life just seems too much to handle. Maybe you've lost a job or a marriage. Maybe you're fighting what feels like overwhelming obstacles at work. Maybe you feel as though you just can't make it through another day. If you're lucky, you'll have someone there to offer a word of encouragement, to tell you that it's okay, that they have faith in you. The right bit of encouragement in the darkest of times can make all the difference.

The great Dodgers second baseman Jackie Robinson came to the major leagues in 1947. We celebrate Robinson because, along with being a gifted athlete, he broke the color barrier in baseball. What we often forget, or don't know, is the abuse he initially took. Despite his prowess as a ball player, during that first summer in New York, the crowds regularly booed, jeered and verbally abused him with racial epithets.

As a matter of course, Robinson refused to let the abuse rattle him by channeling his energy into more aggressive play. But one day he made an error on a routine play. The crowd erupted with hissing and booing. Normally, he would have shrugged it off. But that day, the ridicule and the jeers didn't stop but went on for what seemed like forever.

Jackie stood at second base, humiliated. He felt frozen, unable to move. Then Pee Wee Reese, the Dodgers shortstop, walked up to Robinson, reached out his arm, and put it around Jackie's shoulder. Together they faced the crowd. Together they waited, Reese glaring up at the stands, until the crowd fell silent.

Reese and Robinson. Together they went on to become a great double-play combination, together they helped the Dodgers win many pennants. But Jackie always looked back on that day as a pivotal moment. He said: "That day Pee Wee saved my career."

Use the power of affirmation

Become a "balcony person" for family, friends and co-workers. Like Jim Boone, learn to listen with all your attention. Find ways to catch them doing something right. Don't wait for perfection. Give others honest compliments regularly for doing something good, even if it isn't perfect. Work overtime, as Garnett Griffiths did, to see not only who someone is but also what they have in them to become.

At the very least, you'll brighten someone's day. At the most you may change a life. And maybe someday, just when you least expect it but need it most, you'll look over your shoulder and see your own balcony is full.

Questions for discussion:

- Think of a balcony person in your life. Take a few minutes to write a note or call the person to tell them how much they've done for you.
- Who in your life needs a balcony person? Could you become one for them?
- Try the active listening techniques outlined in this chapter at work or with friends and family. See what effect it has.
- Try practicing affirmation by giving five honest compliments in the next three days.

For more on affirmation:

- Watch the 1975 movie "One Flew Over the Cuckoo's Nest" or read the original 1962 book by Ken Kesey. See how Randal McMurphy changes the lives of mental institution inmates through a rough brand of affirmation in themselves, independence and life.

CHAPTER 6

The Power of Laughter

"Laughter is the shortest distance between two people."
—Victor Borge

It was Community Talent Night, and the school gym was jammed. Farmers had finished their chores early. Shopkeepers had closed before the usual hour. Everyone had gobbled their supper so they could get a good seat. The buzz throughout the gymnasium was, "What do you think Polly will do?"

Every year, Polly Lindquist, our own beloved, copper-haired version of Lucille Ball at her wackiest—the most resourceful, entertaining, hysterically funny woman any of us knew personally—did something to shock and delight. She had already been a clown, a vampire and a baby. What would she do tonight?

The ruby-colored velvet stage curtains slid open, the requisite nervous coughing subsided, and the show began. Several acts followed, including singers and instrumentalists. Every act was good, remarkably good, for a town as small as Clemons, Iowa. But where was Polly? Had she taken sick?

Then the house lights went up, and we heard her voice from the back of the room. She spoke with a strong Hungarian accent. What we saw when we should have seen Polly was the caricature of a gypsy fortune-teller. A long, tousled black wig hid her bright hair. Somehow her costume; low cut white blouse with puffy sleeves, garish skirt and tightly-cinched sash; gave her lanky frame a seductive shape. Lots of stage makeup, false eyelashes, bright red lips and enormous hoop earrings transformed our Polly into a raffish replica of Marlene Dietrich in the old movie "Golden Earrings".

As she came down the center aisle, she stopped and grabbed hands, telling rapid-fire fortunes at the top of her voice. Using a farmer's bald head as an impromptu crystal ball, she said "I see a hair stylist in your future," bringing the house down. She managed to capitalize with hilarity but not cruelty on the quirks and peccadilloes of person after person. By the time she reached the front row, we were all intoxicated with laughter.

Again Polly had made the evening. Because of her, we went home, and to bed, chuckling.

But you had to wonder how Polly felt, driving home by herself in her outlandish costume, checking her sleeping son and daughter, thanking the friend who had spent the evening with Pat. How did Polly feel knowing she'd made so many of us happy when so much of her life had gone sour?

Polly's husband, Pat, had Multiple Sclerosis. Polly and the children she and Pat had adopted as babies watched as he went from a strapping, handsome businessman to someone who became bed-ridden and eventually could neither move nor speak.

How did Polly handle the tragedy in her life? First, by not complaining, even though no one would have blamed her if she did. But she never indicated that she felt sorry for herself. And always Polly made us laugh. With humor, she made our lives better. With humor, she made her life bearable.

Polly hosted more children's parties than any of the other parents in town. Pat was never shunted aside. His bed was right off the living room. We kids would watch television in his room. We performed crazy antics, had make-your-own-pizza parties and danced to old 45s at his bedside.

If you're lucky, you know a Polly—a person who brings laughter and joy to everyone they know, even if they themselves are hurting. And that's the lesson. Regardless of how much we plan and work, the only thing we really get to control is how we react to what life dishes up.

You don't need to be the life of the party or a natural comedian; you just need to understand the power of laughter and put it to good use.

Laughter is about enjoying life

Tune into NBC on any weekday afternoon, and you'll see the power of laughter. Comedienne Ellen Degeneres opens her talk show every day with something simple, fun and powerful. She dances her way from the back of the studio to the set where she'll spend the next hour hosting the show. Ellen is not a great dancer, but dancing in itself is not the point of the opening of the show. Soon the entire audience joins her in grooving to the beat. The simple act opens up everyone—the studio audience and those watching from home—to laugh and have a good time. Ellen enjoys life, and her audiences therefore enjoy watching her show.

People who laugh do more than make others laugh. They make them feel welcome and accepted.

And this kind of therapeutic laughter has the power to bond us together as people. In her personal blog Marti Smith wrote, "Don't you love being in a group that has at least one or two people who love to laugh? Don't you feel more loved . . . . in a group of people like that? Don't you feel closer to people with whom you regularly laugh? It's like glue!" [1]

Laughter is good for you

Early on, our father chose humor as a way to deal with tough times. Thanks to him our family never lacked for laughter. We used it to celebrate, to heal and sometimes, even to grieve. In the darkest of times, Dad could cleanse your soul with a quip or joke followed by a rich chuckle at his own wit.

He often said, "If you're feeling bad, do something nice for someone else. Make them laugh."

Finally a few years ago, he knew he needed a special fix of doing something nice. After losing his wife of 66 years and dealing with health issues of his own, he obviously wasn't feeling great. That's no doubt why he asked us to take him on a driving pilgrimage back to see a childhood friend who was living as a shut-in in northern Wisconsin.

Alida Bolander-French was a charming, sweet soul Dad had grown up with in that part of the world. She and her sister had been the undeniable beauties of Town Corner Township, and she could still light up a room. Both families had homesteaded there, but unlike many, she never left. She could barely see or walk and was in an assisted-living home. Yet despite being two years his senior, her memory and zest for life matched Dad's.

The years melted away as the two old friends reminisced.

Between them, they'd lost two spouses, a son, ten brothers and sisters and most of their lifelong friends. They'd lived through everything the land and the times could throw at them. And yet the indomitable spirits of these two survivors swelled to fill the room with their good humor.

They happily retold old stories, such as when Mrs. Gustuffson came face to face with a bear in a raspberry patch and fled to a neighbor's home to get help—unsuccessfully because she'd lapsed into Norwegian.

They guffawed at the time a neighbor finally tired of spending his days behind a slow-moving, flatulent workhorse. He readied a wooden match and at the next outburst lit it and pushed it into the offending cloud. The resulting explosion not only galvanized the animal, it carried the horse, plow and startled plowman across two fence lines, a creek and into a blueberry bog.

Throughout the afternoon, they jibed, joked and flirted and together wielded the magic that had allowed them to grow to a vibrant old age.

They laughed. Oh, how they laughed.

And with glistening eyes, we laughed with them.

What Dad and Alida knew instinctively science has proven.

In Dr. Norman Cousins' book Anatomy of an Illness, the author describes how watching, and laughing at, Marx Brothers movies helped him recover from a life-threatening tissue disease. "I was greatly elated by the discovery that there is a physiological basis for the ancient theory that laughter is good medicine." he wrote. [2]

Two University of Maryland Medical Center studies link laughter to heart health. The first showed that those with heart disease were forty percent less likely to laugh than those of the same age without heart disease. The second showed that laughter helped open up blood vessels that may have become dangerously narrowed because of stress. [3]

No doubt you've read of other studies showing that the mini-vacation of laughter is good for the lungs, increases metabolism, releases pain-killing endorphins, and reduces muscle tension and high blood pressure.

Laughter is good for business

Arne Hoel (pronounced "hole") understands the power of laughter. As the CEO of Swift Communications he had the serious job of running a multi-million dollar media company. While some in his position lead with their egos, he used self-deprecating humor to put others at ease and to draw out their opinions. Many in his position act as if they're the smartest person in the room, even when they aren't. Joke-telling Arne seldom acts as though he thinks he's the smartest man in the room, even though he often is. As a member of the Swift management team I got to watch firsthand as this tall Norwegian used his humor-filled easy-going style to bring out the best of those around him. The rest of us didn't have to worry about how to negotiate around his ego and instead could feel comfortable to spend our time on doing our best in an open, friendly atmosphere. His humor could lighten any situation. This, after all, is the man who started a corporate meeting on a new e-mail system by admitting he had approved a naming system that used the first initial combined with the last name—even though his address would read phonetically as "A-hole."

"I guess we believe in truth in advertising," he quipped.

One of the Greeley Tribune's tenets was "We work too hard not to have a good time." Of course the staff faced the pressure of daily deadlines along with the serious task of reporting some very sad stories. On top of that there was the natural friction that can happen in any workplace. Still, freed by the comfort that comes with working in a place based on trust and mutual respect, and inspired by the example of department heads and longtime employees, even the newest staffer soon learned it was OK to laugh.

Not everyone thought it was a wonderful thing. I remember a stern-faced businesswoman who stuck her head in my office door and asked, "Do you know what they're doing out here? They're laughing!"

She obviously didn't appreciate the situation, but it was music to my ears. Every good manager knows that happy people are not only more fun to work with, they're more productive, are appreciated by customers, tend to stay with the company, and help recruit others just like themselves. They also know that laughter from a happy staff is an indication of a healthy, successful place. The Tribune staff excelled by most any industry measure and ultimately proved that laughter is simply good for business.

Laughter is a gift

Our Aunt Deane was larger than life in more ways than one. At barely five feet, she was a juggernaut of energy. Educator, church volunteer, Red Cross director, program organizer, mother and farm wife, she packed life with the work of three or four people.

She was also far from dainty. Her girth showed that she appreciated her own fabulous cooking that featured the butter and cream from their dairy farm.

But the biggest thing about Aunt Deane was her laugh. A wonderful teller of stories, her own laughter was a large part of the performance. She'd usually begin to get "tickled" about halfway through a tale and begin to chuckle. Slowly the movement that began in her belly would resonate through the rest of her considerable flesh until her entire body would reverberate with the guffawing conclusion that would bring down the house.

Her infectious good humor never failed to brighten the days of those around her. Smart and insightful, she could use her sardonic wit to take the sting out of a burned finger or to reprimand an errant schoolboy. Sometimes she'd use it to heal relationships.

She loved to tell the story about the road trip she and Uncle Harold took with our parents. Newlyweds all, they could afford only one small motel room between them, so it was decided the girls would sleep there while their husbands would bed-down in the car. That night, Aunt Deane was the first to try out the room's compact bathtub. She wedged herself in and turned on the water. Shortly thereafter she called her sister-in-law into the room. There was a problem. The water was only filling the front half of the tub. The back half was bone-dry thanks to a dam created by Aunt Deane's body. Both women began to giggle. Deane tried to stand up but the water had created a suction that held her fast. She began her trademark laugh as Mom pitched in to pull for all she was worth.

The story goes that after much effort, Deane finally came flying out with the sound of an oversized cork popping out of a bottle only to collapse with Mom on the bathroom floor, both overcome with seizures of laughter.

Despite the occasional friction the sisters-in-law would inevitably encounter over the next 60 years, Deane could always smooth things over and make our mother smile by telling that story.

Our aunt understood the power of being able to laugh at oneself. In practice, that talent helps others lighten up, makes you approachable, and at the very heart of things, makes others comfortable because you obviously are comfortable with yourself.

Laugh every day

Doesn't it seem that people are getting grumpier?

Denver's Cherry Creek is one of those charming, revitalized urban areas littered with smart shops, restaurants and galleries. Summer weekends find up-scale couples lounging at outdoor cafés or pushing baby strollers. You'd think this idyllic place would ring with laughter. Instead during a recent summer afternoon it seemed more likely to reverberate with angry horns: there was the blonde teenager in her black BMW who paused from texting to honk at the delivery guy taking too much time in the crosswalk. There was the businessman in sunglasses who laid on his Mercedes' horn when the lady in the Volvo shot into a parking spot he was waiting for. In fact car horns were braying their owners' displeasure at crosswalks and corners throughout the area. There in that beautiful, up-scale enclave, people just didn't seem to be happy. Of course, it's not just a disease of the rich. You'll find harried, stern-faced people on any street corner in America. Maybe you're one of them.

Have you ever asked yourself what's wrong? As Americans, we enjoy the most luxurious lifestyle the world has ever seen. We've countless time-saving devices and yet it seems we just can't get caught up. We have so much that others in the world envy: cars, cell phones, TVs, closets full of clothes, dry sturdy homes and refrigerators full of food. But where's the joy? For all our wealth, we can't seem to get enough. While those in other countries save—the Japanese put away 20 percent of their incomes, the Germans and English save

15 percent—Americans have a negative saving rate of 2.2 percent. [4] That means despite the efforts by many to save for retirement, we as a nation, are spending more than we make.

When economist John Kenneth Galbraith wrote "The Affluent Society," he talked about a "Dependence Effect." In reference to the acquisition of material goods, he wrote, "The more wants that are satisfied, the more new ones are born." [5] He went on to liken the consumer to a squirrel on a treadmill—forever running after the latest material doo-dad.

Is it any wonder we seem to have turned into those squirrels that run faster and faster every day without ever feeling happy about it?

So what should you do?

Polly would probably suggest you forget forking out the cash for a new Playstation and instead invite your kids and their friends to a pizza party, the kind where they make it themselves.

Our father would probably counsel you to do something nice for someone else.

Aunt Deane might suggest a recipe for squirrel stew.

All would tell you to just lighten up.

There are times when choosing laughter can mean choosing life—choosing life literally, because the health benefits of laughter are so well-documented. But deciding to laugh when you least feel like it, making the conscious choice to look at the absurdity of a tense situation, also can save not only a momentary situation. Choosing to laugh can save your job, your relationships, even your marriage.

"He who laughs lasts," George Bernard Shaw wrote. And he was right. Laughter can be one of your most potent life survival techniques.

Our friend Jo Walker was the wife of a military officer who moved his family around the world with discomforting regularity. I once asked how she managed to stay so happy during their 40-plus years of marriage. "I chose to look at the absurdity of situations that could have made me feel sad, angry or depressed," she said. "Faced with a desperate situation, I laughed. Sometimes I cried, too, but I made myself laugh. And with laughter, my equilibrium was restored. If you can still laugh, it means you haven't lost your hope."

Laughter and hope are closely linked. When you're in a tight place—in an argument with your spouse, child, a friend or a co-worker—or if an angry stranger for some reason accosts you, stop. Take a minute. Consider the situation from a vantage point far outside yourself. Is there anything in this situation that might be construed as even faintly humorous? If the answer is yes, grab hold of it. Focus on it. See the humor. Build on the humor. Force yourself to smile. A smile can lead to a chuckle. A chuckle can lead to genuine laughter. And when that happens, you have created for yourself an alternative response to an unhappy situation.

Without laughter, we become tight like the strings of an over-tuned guitar. Laughter is a device we have to loosen the strings of our personality. When you're in the clinches, try laughter. It can help save a situation, a relationship and your health.

Choose laughter, choose life.

Questions for discussion:

- Do you know someone who always seems to find a way to laugh about things? How do you think they do that? How do other people react to them?
- What's happened to you in the past three days that you probably could have laughed about but didn't? Make a list of amusing things.
- Laughter is almost always just under the surface waiting to break out. To prove this, play the Ha-Ha game with friends or family. Have one first person lie down on the floor, the second should lie down and put their head on the first person's stomach. The third will lie down with their head on the second person's stomach and so on. Have the first person loudly say "Ha!" The second will say "Ha! Ha!" the third "Ha! Ha! Ha!"

and so on. You'll have people roaring before they finish the line. Want to make it more interesting? Tell people that no matter what happens, they can't laugh during the game, and see if they can do it.

For more on laughter:

- Rent a comedy or watch one on TV (we happen to love the 1933 Marx Brothers classic, "Duck Soup"). Instead of sitting quietly, laugh out loud when you find something amusing. You may be a little self-conscious at first, but see how you feel by the time you finish.

CHAPTER 7

The Power of Community

"The more connected we are, the safer we are."
—Robert Johansen, Executive Director,
Institute for the Future

The little old widow is getting a home permanent. She's smiling—not just because she's having her hair done in her kitchen, but because Marie Van Metre, the pretty lady doing the work is such a joy to be with. Marie is in her late forties but looks years younger. She has an ageless face, petal soft skin, endearing dimples and a Cupid's bow mouth. But it's the eyes that tell the tale. They're huge, bright blue and sparkle as though she has a great story she can't wait to share. Her infectious laugh lights up the room.

She really didn't have time to help Catherine with her hair today. Her work as town post-mistress keeps her busy enough. Then there's the church choir practice she needs to lead later tonight, not to mention running errands for Aunt Madie or the casserole she plans to make for poor Mrs. Behrens, who's been down with the flu. Of course, she needs to plan dinner for her family and the nice new doctor and his wife who are staying with them until they get settled. Throw in the regular chores of being a wife and mother, and she has plenty to keep her busy.

But Catherine doesn't know all that. Marie makes her feel like doing her hair is the most important thing in the world. Then with a dazzling smile, she's finished and out the door. Picture her charging up the street on a Saturday morning in mid-December. It's snowing. Not a blizzard; no wind. One of those picturesque snows when the flakes descend like little white butterflies. The snow is heavy and wet and it's piling up fast. Everybody's out getting their shopping done early so they can hole up at home and forgo braving the roads later.

Ever resourceful, Marie trumps the weather by carrying of all things a parasol. Who ever heard of anyone carrying a parasol in a snowstorm? But here's Marie—coat, hat, gloves, galoshes and this bit of unlikely flowered feminine frippery her armor against the elements.

She scurries along, as trim, erect and spritely as Tinker Bell on an errand for Peter. She might have, in Paul Simon's words, diamonds on her shoes so lightly does she trip through the gathering snow. And like a diamond, her personality sparkles, beams, entrancing everyone in sight. She has a quick word for everybody. Everybody's happy to see her. A couple of minutes' chat with Marie makes you forget the storm and glow with warmth despite the cold.

Marie doesn't mind her busy days. After all, it's what you do when you're part of a community.

Wouldn't we all like to have a Marie Van Metre in our lives? Someone with a quick smile and glowing personality to invite us to parties, take care of our children when we're out of town, welcome us when we've no place else to stay, comfort us with food and prayers when we're down and run errands for us when we're old. We all want friends to count on in the best and worst of times.

Of course what we all really want is not just one super-friend but rather the comfort of being in a community of people who will do all of that for us. From the dawn of recorded history, people have naturally thrived in communities: the family unit, the extended family, clans, tribes, towns, cities and nations. Whatever the size, people have automatically seen themselves, defined themselves, in terms of some group.

Marie and her husband, Earl, were the heart and soul, and often the brains, of our little community. They served on nearly every town committee and chaired most. More importantly, they were always doing things for others. With wit and all the right instincts about people and organizations, they helped keep our town moving in a positive direction for close to fifty years.

They knew everyone needs to feel as though they belong to something. They also knew an important secret: The best communities are those we help build ourselves.

Community as a safety net

Our community included our hometown of Clemons and the surrounding farmland that stretched east and west along Minerva Valley. Whenever people moved, they didn't hire a mover, people just turned out to help. Friends, relatives and neighbors descended in droves. Trucks in a variety of sizes and descriptions, burdened with possessions, cavalcaded down rutted gravel roads and descended on the new house. All the movers sat down to a communal hot meal at noon provided, again, by the neighbors.

If a farmer fell ill at planting or harvest time, he didn't have to worry about his crop, or his wife and children. Neighbors on their bright red International Harvester Farmalls and bright green John Deeres would roar up the lane and tear into the rich black loam in April or May and reap the soil's amazing produce of corn and soy beans in October.

Community was everywhere and apparent day in, day out and year in, year out. Community meant people caring for people and not being too proud to depend on each other when times were tough. Nobody thought it strange that we needed each other. Of course, we needed each other. How else can people live together? How else can people build a nation together?

Sure, some of us couldn't stand each other. We knew of one or two life feuds, but they were the exception. Mostly we worked hard at getting along. The Depression spawned a generation of pack rats. You never wanted to throw anything away because you never knew when you might need it. In the same way, we knew we never wanted to casually throw away a relationship because we needed the strength and support we got from each other. Our mother always said, "I'd rather have the good will of a dog than the bad," and she applied that careful diplomacy with everyone she knew.

We didn't question our interdependency. We didn't have any choice. We were stuck with each other, rooted to the same rich chunk of prairie topsoil. We belonged to each other. Mostly we were fiercely loyal. Mostly, although we were too reserved to say it, we loved each other.

Communities are intentional

Unfortunately, the kind of community we experienced as kids is rare today. That's too bad because the psychological and physical health benefits to living in such forms of highly-connected community have been well documented.

In his book "Bowling Alone," Harvard professor Robert Putnam wrote that the best established benefit of social connectedness is health and well-being. Since 2000, when Putnam's book was published, data continues to accrue reinforcing the message: The more integrated with some form of community we are, the less likely we are to experience colds, heart attacks, strokes, cancer, depression, and premature death of all sorts. "Such protections," writes Putnam, "have been confirmed for close family ties, for friendship networks, for participation in social events, and even for simple affiliation with religious and other civic associations." [1]

The opposite of social connectedness—social alienation—has been proven to have equally profound negative results. Putnam goes on to say that dozens of studies in the U.S., Japan and Scandinavia show that people who are socially disconnected are two to five times more likely to die of all causes.

Our nation has moved away from the kind of community we knew and valued. After the Second World War, the returning U.S. troops often did not settle down in their hometowns. After the late-1940s, Americans picked up and moved across the country for jobs, opportunities and new experiences.

Community in its old-fashioned form began to dissolve.

From 1974 to 1998, the frequency with which Americans spent a social evening with neighbors fell by about one-third. In "Bowling Alone," Putnam delineated the disintegration of the American social fabric. He concluded that neighborhood ties are less than half as strong in today's America as they were in the 1950s.

Despite the disintegration of community, we still need it. We were not designed to live alone and dependent only on our own resources, but in community. Even in a country of individuals such as ours where self-reliance and self-confidence are prized national attributes, people still need people. We need each other for support, for wisdom, for perspective, for accountability, for encouragement along the way of our lives.

Even as Putnam and other sociologists decried the collapse of community and the rise of alienation in our country, a new kind of community experience is gaining momentum. Much of it has come via the Internet with an ever-evolving host of social networking sites. All are new kinds of community.

This new kind of community helped elect Barrack Obama in the 2008 presidential election. Social networking by Internet, with its communication capabilities and aggressive database development, enabled the Obama campaign to raise money, organize locally and fight the opposition. As a result, Obama found himself with more than a political base. He had a database, millions of names of supporters who can be engaged almost instantly. Politics in this country were forever changed.

Still, we need the old kind of community where you can have eye contact, touch, share the same environment, share the physical moment. A psychologist once said that for optimum health we need eight hugs a day!

Community happens in crisis

Sometimes a community will show up just when you need it most. That's what happened to Alan and Sara Karnitz. I've known Alan ever since he started at the Tribune as a goofy, gangly intern.

With a huge grin and unsinkable—if slightly off-center—sense of humor, he was also a brilliant designer and rose quickly through the ranks to become the director of the department. More comfortable talking about his beloved Green Bay Packers than he was with women, we were all pleasantly surprised when he married the pretty, self-confident Sara.

Tragically one night, their newlywed heaven turned into a private hell when a man with a shotgun burst into their house. He was looking for his estranged wife, Nikki, who was there with Sara's brother, Sam. Alan and Sara ran as shots roared through the night. They came back to find Nikki bleeding to death on the floor. They tried to save her but failed. Sam had two wounds but was alive.

Sam eventually began to recover, but the tough times were just beginning for Alan and Sara. While trying to sort out the horror of that night, they had something else to grieve over—the miscarriage of their first child. Both dealt with shock and depression. By his own admission Alan's was the worst.

A victim's advocate put them in touch with the local Faith Community Service Fund. They wanted to help the Karnitzes erase the horrors they'd lived through. They offered to help remodel their home. Shortly after that, members of the Christ Community Church invited them for dinner. Over an informal potluck, they also offered money and volunteers for the project.

As quoted in a Greeley Tribune story, Alan said, "So many people helped us unconditionally. They knew we were hurting, and they just wanted to help. It was amazing." [2]

Alan, Sara and their new community of friends ripped apart the inside of their house and the memories that went with it.

Today the couple has weathered their storm. They have loads of new friends who visit them often in their freshly remodeled home. Healing also has come through another new beginning—the birth of Faith Maureen Karnitz.

You are the beginning of your own community

Community doesn't just happen without effort. We have to be willing to give, to sometimes risk making ourselves vulnerable. And running like a golden thread, binding us one to another in community, are the twin themes of trust and respect. They are what keep a community healthy, be it family, church, institution, organization of any kind. Without trust and respect, none of us can feel safe. And when we feel safe, we do our best work and become our best selves. It all begins with you.

Want more friends? Take a lesson from Tonya Lyons, who sees so many people when she volunteers up to twenty hours a week with the local chamber and Jaycees. That's in addition to everyone she works with at her full-time job helping the developmentally disabled. Then there are the friends/students at her dance studio. A dancer for most of her twenty-nine years, she took up belly dancing because she loved it and because it was easier for her to handle than some other dance forms. She has rheumatoid arthritis and a newly diagnosed disease that's slowly destroying some of her cells. While others with less disability may find themselves lonely at home, Tonya has built a huge community of friends. [3]

Want good neighbors? Be the first to show up with a plate of cookies for the new move-ins. If you can, help a neighbor pull some weeds or shovel snow. Offer to run an errand or two for them if they're under the weather or to keep an eye on their place when they're out of town. Of course, there are some who just want to be left alone, but most will appreciate the gesture. Many, given time, will return the favor.

Lonely in retirement? Take Ken Kisselman's lead and volunteer at the local hospital. Ken is a cancer survivor who is always there to help those who are dealing with the disease, whether laughing with them, crying with them or just listening. [4]

Want to attend more parties? Throw some yourself.

Need someone to lean on in tough times? Start by reaching out to others who are facing their own challenges, and just like Earl and Marie Van Metre, you may just find the favor returned.

You can hear Marie's infectious laughter as soon as you walk in from the porch. This time, she's the one getting the permanent. There she is, chattering away in the kitchen, towel on her shoulder and curlers in her hair. Despite her 80-plus years, her personality still lights up the room. Her younger friend Laureen doesn't say much, but that's OK. Marie fills in the conversation for both of them.

Just as they're finishing up, Woody's face pops around the back door. "Got the fence fixed!" he booms in his lusty baritone. "Think I'll need to take a look at that back roof spout next week."

Marie rewards each with one of her sparkling smiles, and they leave happily to go tend to their own families. They don't mind doing things for the Van Metres. They've helped so many people over the years it's nice to be able to do something for them.

Besides, it's what you do when you're part of a community.

Questions for discussion:

- How would you define community?
- Have you experienced any of the kinds of community described in this chapter?

- Have you experienced a negative community? If so, what was it like? What were the underlying causes?
- If you're not in a healthy community now, list three things you could do to help create one.

For more about community:

- Read "Bowling Alone" by Robert D. Putnam.
- Watch the 1946 film classic "It's a Wonderful Life" to be reminded of how a community you helped build can pay you back.

CHAPTER 8

The Power of Humility

"Humility must always be the portion of any man who receives
acclaim earned in the blood of his followers and
the sacrifices of his friends."
—Dwight D. Eisenhower

Everything felt better when Reverend Proctor was there.
One look at his bald, gently rotund form bouncing
through the hospital room door calmed the fears of the most anxious
patient. He could bound late into a church meeting frozen by conflict
and, in a few minutes, with a whimsical phrase and light-hearted
banter, thaw the tension and forge resolution.

And when he marched down the aisle on Sunday mornings for the
ten o'clock service, you felt parishioners breathing easier and relaxing
a little from the tensions of the week. As one man put it: "God's in
His heaven, Lester Proctor's going to preach. All may not be well with
the world, but with Lester here, it's a whole lot better."

To us boys, he was not only a stand-in for God but also the
personification of good will, hope and wisdom.

For all these reasons, and more, the awful end to his ministry
among us traumatized not only our family but also our normally
close-knit community.

It started with the one conflict Lester Proctor couldn't resolve: an argument about which organ to buy as part of the church renovation. He made an enemy; some said the first enemy he'd ever had in his fifty-plus years. The enemy proved implacable, relentless and creative in his determination to get rid of the pastor. A brush fire of accusations and damning half-truths flamed through the congregation, burning away trust in the pastor and trust in each other. The church, finally, was split.

We were a Congregational church, meaning the congregation voted annually on whether or not to retain the pastor for another year. What always had been a vote of total confidence now eroded. It took three years, but on the third annual vote, Lester was out. In the end, only our parents and a handful of other loyalists stood with our friend.

The fabric of our church community was temporarily destroyed, our boyhood faith in organized religion temporarily shattered with it.

Lester was shattered, too. But he took the never-expected blow with stoic grace. Word had it that in church board meetings he answered accusations quietly and truthfully. When the final vote came that Sunday morning, he simply walked through the rows of people who had been his cherished flock and his friends, and to whom he had ministered with boundless caring and compassion, and out the door. Lester never publicly defended himself. He'd given his best years to these people, and they were casting him aside, but he never showed anger, bitterness or resentment. Like Jesus when accused before Pilate, Lester was quiet in the face of his accusers.

It was the worst day in the hundred-year history of our church. Lifetime friendships were frayed, some broken. But the pastor did nothing to aggravate the situation.

He never entered the church again. But he kept his family in town. They lived in a house occupied by his wife's family since pioneer days. Mrs. Proctor kept her job as high school English teacher.

Finally, in less than a year, Lester received a call from another church. It was a Friends church. Lester wasn't a Quaker, but he was willing to adapt. His new congregation adored him. He served that church until he retired. In all those years, he and his new flock enjoyed a relationship of mutual respect and affection. Crucified by one church, Lester Proctor was resurrected by another. And for us, it was his faith and humility that brought him through.

Humility vs. arrogance

Humility isn't a very popular trait. It has a bad rap in our culture. Little prized in the public arena, it's too often equated with weakness, submissiveness, the inability or unwillingness to take care of ourselves. "Stand up for yourself. Don't let anybody run over you," our parents told us. And rightly so.

But when we say humility, we don't mean the kind of cringing, false self-abasement indulged in by Bob Cratchet, Scrooge's bookkeeper in "A Christmas Carol." What we recommend is the kind of humility based on inner strength and self-confidence. A kind of humility that says I don't need to force myself forward or push myself ahead of others, because my natural talents and ability will make a place for me.

All too often, we see the opposite. We see the attitude that says, "Out of my way. I'm here to grab my piece of the action. I'm here to win—at any cost, even if I have to walk over people to do it."

That's arrogance, pride, the opposite of humility. To further understand the meaning of genuine humility, consider other antonyms: conceit, condescension, haughtiness, insolence, presumption, self-importance and self-satisfaction.

What is needed but sorely missing in many controversies in today's world—in politics, business, the economy, international affairs and interpersonal relationships—is the exact opposite of arrogance and pride. What we desperately need is a spirit of humility.

Humility isn't blind

Pride blinds us—to the needs of people around us, to the wisdom we can learn from life and other people, to our part in a conflicted situation. Pride blinds us to reality.

That's why we've seen U. S. presidents in our lifetime perform acts they would never have committed had they not been isolated from reality by pride. Without pride we would never have heard of the break-in at a hotel named Watergate, an intern named Monica Lewinsky, or what was to be just a 12-month military operation in a place called Iraq.

The same thing happens with leaders at every level of prominence and responsibility. Gifted, looked up to, entrusted with authority, when pride blinds them to the possible effects of their actions, how often we've seen them tumble into the dust of humiliation and obscurity. All because somewhere within themselves they harbored the conviction that they couldn't fail.

Turn to the Bible, and you see the same thing happening generation by generation in the lives of God's people. David, whom the Bible calls "the man after God's own heart," became the greatest king of his people. Puffed up with the pride of success and power, isolated as any modern political ruler, David sent Bathsheba's husband to be killed in front line combat so he could possess the beauty himself. In the end, the Lord takes the son of their union and three of his other sons.

Throughout history, in positions of leadership in every field of endeavor, in the lives of people we all know, we see how pride blinds, how pride destroys. It destroys careers, marriages, friendships, partnerships and lives.

The case could be made that the financial collapse in 2008 was spawned in part from the twin evils of greed and pride. Certainly both drove financial giants Bear Sterns, Lehman Brothers and others over the brink to a financial ruin that began in the U.S. and spread around the globe.

None of us is immune to pride. It's a potential danger lurking always within each of us. That's why the Bible says, "The beginning of sin is pride."

Humility is based on strength

Humility is seldom discussed in business circles; in many, it's considered a weakness. Those people confuse self-importance with strength and arrogance with leadership.

Some successful CEOs seem to be closer to egocentric movie stars than business leaders. Flamboyant types like Donald Trump and Martha Stewart may have accomplished much on the strength of their personalities, but experts tell us that's often the exception to the norm. In his best-selling book "Good to Great," Jim Collins studies why some businesses catapulted past competitors to greatness. In it, he profiled "Level 5 Leaders" who, without exception, were at the helm of every company on the list. He wrote this type of leader was ". . . an individual who blends extreme personal humility with intense professional will." [1]

"It's not that the Level 5 leaders have no ego or self-interest," Collins writes. "Indeed, they are incredibly ambitious—but their ambition is first and foremost for the institution, not themselves."

One of the most famous examples of a Level 5 manager is Abraham Lincoln. Shortly after being elected, he had the humility to know the country would need the talents of some of his most bitter rivals for the presidency. He also had the strength to invite them to serve on his cabinet.

Many politicians would have used their first inaugural address to trumpet their victory and to vilify their enemies in the South. Instead, he sent them a love letter, "We are not enemies but friends. We must not be enemies. Though passion may have strained, it must not break our bonds of affection. The mystic chords of memory, stretching from every battlefield, and patriot grave, to every living heart and hearthstone, all over this broad land, will yet swell the chorus of the Nation, when again touched, as surely they will be, by the better angels of our nature."

Lincoln was humble enough to appreciate the gravity of the task before him and strong enough to lead our nation through some of our darkest days.

If an iconic leader like Lincoln can find success through humility, perhaps we can, too.

Humility and the teachable spirit

Even when we succumb to the worst kind of pride, there's a way out. The way out is humility. That doesn't mean being servile or standing for nothing. It's a humility based not on weakness, but on the strength of being open to new things.

Many years ago, I had the good fortune to under study a retired Baptist minister. John Hamrich was a huge, slow moving man with a rumbling south Georgia drawl. John had spent his adult life ministering to people. Eager to learn everything I could from this deeply spiritual man, I pummeled him with questions. What did he consider the most desirable trait a person can possess? He said: "Far and away, a teachable spirit. Without a teachable spirit, you can go through life without learning, without maturing; basically staying the same as you started. But with a teachable spirit, you can make the most of life's teachings. You can see life for the lesson book it's meant to be for all of us. You can grow, evolve, and become increasingly your best self—the self you were meant to be."

Humility can be learned

Some of us with less-than teachable spirits, if we learn humility at all, learn it the hard way—by the storms and battering of life.

It was 1985, and suddenly the party was over in Natchez, Mississippi. That was too bad because it was a town that loved its parties. Perched on the bluffs overlooking the Mississippi River, it had first been a stop for river boatmen and adventurers—its rollicking "Under the Hill" saloons and brothels became infamous throughout the American West. Later the verdant croplands on the Louisiana side of the river blossomed with cotton plantations, and Natchez became the playground for the outrageously wealthy. The pre-Civil War mansions buzzed with soirees featuring hoop-skirted belles who sipped French champagne and fluttered their fans at the South's most eligible bachelors.

Of course the Civil War changed all that. The following long years of reconstruction were tough and the new century only brought the Depression and a further downturn in fortunes. But then oil was discovered under the cotton fields and the gusher of new wealth flooded the city with money. Once again the verandas and parlors were alive with the sound of revelry and popping corks.

Then came the bust of 1985 when petroleum prices plummeted. Thriving oil towns from Canada to West Texas changed overnight, Natchez among them. Businesses, some more than a hundred years old, closed at an alarming rate. Those left standing struggled to stay afloat.

Even the city's 150-year-old daily newspaper, the Natchez Democrat, was rocked. A newspaper lives on its advertising dollars, and closed businesses don't advertise. As a young management team, in the years prior, we'd reveled in huge revenue gains and the big bonuses we got as a result. We were selling lots of papers, ad sales were up 25 percent, and we were all making more money than we thought possible. Damn we were good—have some champagne.

Within twelve months of the bust, we'd cut back to publishing six days a week and were facing our third round of layoffs just to make ends meet. We were spending countless hours deciding who would have a job next week before pitching in to cover for those who'd already left.

Have you ever had to look a friend in the eye and tell him his job is gone or spent sleepless nights wondering how your business can pay its bills? Have you ever walked into your office or living room, turned your head to the ceiling and asked, "God, what am I doing here?" Desperation can be crippling.

It was in those dark days that the leadership prayer came to me. I suspect that the simple cry for help has been echoed throughout the ages. My version went like this: "Lord, today help me be the person others need me to be." And I prayed those words daily.

I was foolish enough to think our former success meant I had all the answers. I thought I knew how to run a successful business. Suddenly I realized I hadn't a clue about how to run one that was failing. All I knew was that people were turning to me for answers, for help, for a plan to crawl out of the hole we were in. No matter how hard I worked or how many hours I put in, it seemed as though success, which had come so easily before, slipped through my hands.

If our executive team of precocious twenty-somethings had been honest, we would have admitted that in our minds, previous success was really all about us. How good could we be? But there's no place for arrogance and egos when people are really counting on you.

They want someone who can acknowledge difficulties while still having the strength and courage to help others. They want help in coping with their own problems, and most importantly, they want help making things better for everyone.

Gradually, the situation forced us to understand that success wasn't about us. It was about what we could do for others.

We were pushed out of our self-centered shells and began to talk with employees about ways we could revive the business. We used their ideas to create new plans that were shared with all. We found new, sometimes consciously silly, ways to celebrate and reward people. We laughed with them and sometimes we cried with them.

We worked very hard at trying to be the people they needed us to be.

Eventually the hemorrhaging stopped. There were fewer employees at the newspaper, but amazingly they seemed more engaged and happier with their jobs. Productivity soared. The company began to sell even more papers with award-winning journalism, and while other area businesses continued to struggle, the sales charts in the paper's ad department began to head up.

A happy byproduct was that a handful of young newspaper managers had taken the first steps toward becoming real leaders—leaders who had been humbled through hardship.

Humility listens

Media bashing is a popular sport. One need only see the pack of rabid journalists surrounding the latest victim of some tragedy to see why. Don't you cringe when some self-important broadcaster shoves a microphone in the face of a mother who's just lost a child in a horrific accident and asks, "How do you feel?" It's tough to think about humility when members of the media look like preening, self-interested vultures.

Still, I have to defend members of my old profession. There are a great many journalists who care deeply about doing the right thing and they do so with dedication, everyday ethics and humility. One of the best examples is Mike Peters. Although he's had plenty of opportunities to go to larger news operations, Mike continues to ply his trade at the newspaper in Greeley, Colorado. Funny, self-deprecating and talented, he's covered many fatalities, including those that were spectacular enough to draw in the Denver network media horde. Often when that circus of trucks, cameras, lights and helicopters fails to get an interview with a grief-stricken family, Mike will quietly get the story.

He does it like this: He calls the family and introduces himself. Usually they know him by reputation so they'll talk without hanging up. Next, in a respectful voice, he says, "I'm so very sorry for your loss. I know this is a tough time for you, but if you'd like to talk, if you'd like to let others know about your loved one's life, I'm happy to listen. If not, I'll go away."

Then they talk to Mike. They talk to him because they want to share their grief and because he listens with such care and humility.

Mike believes people will write their own stories if you listen carefully enough.

Here's an example of Mike's work:

"It rained Monday. A slow, soft drizzle; sad. In most cases it might have been the perfect day to plan a funeral. But not for Bob and Laura Berends, because they knew their daughter was more like a day of sunshine.

"She walked into a room and it brightened," her mother said. "People were drawn to her." Bethany Gibson, 21, died early Friday morning when the motorcycle on which she was a passenger crashed . . . ." [2]

It's that kind of approach that has countless clippings of Mike's stories saved throughout the county. The Berends and others who've found themselves in tragic circumstances have been comforted by the fact there was a journalist of courtesy, compassion and humility to help them tell their story.

Humility comes from tough times

In all our years growing up in Clemons, we never knew a truly prideful or arrogant person. Other character flaws, yes, including one or two who were downright mean-spirited. But those people were extremely rare. The men and women we knew had been tempered and refined by the Great Depression and the war that followed. Dependence on a farm-based economy that depended on the Iowa weather bred a healthy humility. People spent a lot of time talking about the weather. If we could have looked into their hearts, we probably would have seen they spent even more time praying about it.

The people we knew had lost too much—they'd seen people around them lose too much—to walk the risky path of arrogance. If you've been beat down often and decisively enough, you can still spring back, and our people did spring back. But you can't be arrogant.

All too often we misunderstand and even look down on humility as the poor stepchild of society's preferred character traits.

But the wise among us understand something different. They know that true humility is based on self-confidence and character and that there is always something new to be learned if we listen carefully enough. They know humility lets us learn life lessons from failure. They know that arrogance and pride can destroy our hopes and dreams but the power of humility can lead to success in even the toughest of times.

Questions for discussion:

- How would you define humility? Has your definition changed as a result of reading this chapter?
- Have you known someone who possessed the trait of genuine humility? Describe that person. Have they impacted your life in any way? If so, how?
- Why do you think society has traditionally equated humility with weakness? Describe someone you know whose life has been negatively impacted by pride.

For more on humility

- Read a biography of Abraham Lincoln. Consider "Team of Rivals: The Political Genius of Abraham Lincoln" by Doris Kearns Goodwin, or "Lincoln" by David Herbert Donald and see how he balanced humility and strength.
- Watch the 1990 Oscar award-winning movie "Dances with Wolves." How does the main character's life change when he leaves his military training behind and engages a new race of people with humility?

CHAPTER 9

The Power of Love

"The greatest power known to man is that of unconditional
love."
—Harold W. Becker

Barb Martin was crying—nothing dramatic, just an intermittent trail of tears that she swatted impatiently as she continued to talk about her career.

And what a career it had been so far. A mother of three, she'd risen from the ranks in the United States Department of Agriculture to become the coordinator for all the USDA's national animal disease control labs. Those labs are the first line of defense against ugly things like potentially pandemic flu strains and food terrorism. Barb has a top national security clearance and spends a lot of time overseas working with other nations to ensure our U.S. safety net extends beyond our borders. She looks like, and is, one of those coolly professional talking heads we tend to hear from during national crises.

But she was crying as she talked about the person who had changed her life.

"I would never have been able to do this if it weren't for her," she said. "It was her confidence in me that made all the difference."

This was the first time we had met in many years. We'd run with the same pack of kids back in high school—the group that would storm our house at odd hours to refuel from my mother's kitchen. There, Mom dispensed endless amounts of food seasoned with the abiding interest she took in each of us.

Admittedly, Barb had changed a lot since then. She'd been a self-described wallflower in school. Tall, awkward and painfully shy, she probably wouldn't have had much of a social life had she not fallen in with our boisterous, esoteric bunch of musicians, jocks and theater geeks. The thought of taking a speech class back then would have terrified her.

Just a few weeks before our reunion, she'd addressed hundreds on food terrorism at an international conference in Geneva.

We kept in touch after graduation and through college, and no one was happier than I when she ended up marrying one of my best buddies. Then we began a slow drift in different directions. After years of being out of touch, it was a real joy to see the person Barb had become.

Now the normally cool and confident bureaucrat wiped away one last tear as she finished making her point: "Don't you see? She made all the difference. She had confidence in me when no one else did. She made me feel special. I tell you, if it weren't for your mother's love for me, I wouldn't be where I am today."

Love inspires

Friends like Barb could feel the power of our mother's love when they walked into our old farmhouse. First, there was her smile: beaming and radiant, it said seeing them was a wonderful gift. Then there was the food. She loved to cook and bake, and it was nearly impossible for a visitor to make it through her kitchen without being fed. But most important was the interest she took in those she cared about.

Instinctively she'd share more of her time with those who seemed to need it the most. While other friends might be playing games or listening to music, people like Barb would gravitate to our kitchen table. There, mother would begin to work her magic with a glass of milk and some warm cookies. She'd ask questions and then would do an extraordinary thing. She'd listen—really listen.

She'd remember when a big test or state contest was coming and would always ask how they did. Her brilliant blue eyes would sparkle with delight at their triumphs and would crinkle with concern at their worries and fears. She showed an unfailing confidence. "If you put your mind to it, you can do anything," she'd say with unmistakable assurance.

Then, when that confidence propelled them into the unknown to try things they'd never thought possible, she rejoiced in their success. "Oh, I'm so proud of you!" she'd exclaim.

It was like a spring shower to those whose lives were spent in the parched deserts of families built on criticism and neglect. That shower of affection allowed people to bloom. Its power inspired Barb to move beyond her insecurities and self-doubt and achieve a remarkable career.

Love empowers

We use the word love loosely, don't we? I love God. I love my wife, my family, my friends. But I also love a good steak, springtime and fall, working out, going to the beach. I love it when my team wins. We use the word so frequently, sometimes so nonchalantly, we forget that it's the most important word in the language. That's because it's the most important emotion. We're not talking about the shooting-star kind of romantic love that's been idealized for centuries in story and song, we're talking about something deeper, broader and much more powerful. Love is not just a feeling—it's a choice and an action.

Love in our mother was like a force that couldn't be contained. It flowed out of her, nurturing everyone she encountered. If you were part of Mom's great extended circle of family and friends you knew you were loved fully, fairly and without qualification. When you're caught in a force like that, you're changed as Barb was changed. You're empowered.

That's why love is the indispensable emotion—because it has a power like no other power in the universe to change people and situations for good.

Of all the many lessons our mother taught us, the most important was how to love.

Love heals

What our mother knew instinctively, Dr. Dean Ornish has proven in his book "Love and Survival." [1] In it, he gives the scientific basis for the healing power of love.

According to Dr. Ornish, the real epidemic in our culture is what he calls emotional and spiritual heart disease. He describes a profound sense of loneliness, isolation, alienation and depression that is prevalent today. And why? Because the social structures that formerly provided us with a sense of connection and community have in too many instances broken down.

He says we are only now beginning to appreciate what the radical shifts in our society over the past fifty years really mean for us, and for the health of our minds and bodies.

Dr. Ornish gives proof based on scientific studies of how we ought best to live. He says the healthiest people tend to live in close, loving, interdependent groups. They care for one another. They bear each other's burdens. The strong uphold the weak. They create and live a system of mutual truth, acceptance and forbearance.

He quotes a Stanford Medical School study that reports women with cancer who met with a weekly support group—and found there a sense of community and intimacy—lived twice as long as those who had no support group.

It's a breakthrough understanding for the medical community today: that a support group helps offset isolation and loneliness while actually healing our bodies.

Not only does the act of giving love have the ability to heal others, it has the power to heal those who give it. Studies of volunteers have shown that not only do they tend to live longer, they also tend to feel better. Sometimes they actually report feeling a sudden burst of endorphins similar to a "runner's high" while helping others.

Chronic stress can suppress our immune system, opening us up to sickness. On the other hand, expressing the emotions of love and compassion can actually improve our immune systems, not only making us more disease-resistant but also happier and healthier.

We need love

We all want—and need—love. What we often forget is that we have to give away what we want and need. But living our lives as truly loving people is not easy. Learning how to love requires practice. For some of us, like our mother, loving seems to come easily. For others of us, it may not be as natural. We may have to work at it. But it's a proven possibility: We can actually learn how to love. So how do you put the power of love to work in your own life?

Maybe to best understand the how-to of love, we need to consider not what love is but what it is not. If you sincerely want to learn how to love, you can start by carving out of your life everything that doesn't look like love.

And we know what love does not look like, don't we? It doesn't look like being rude or condescending. It doesn't look like road rage. It doesn't look like taking unfair advantage of a waiter or waitress. It doesn't look like trashing someone behind his back or making a cutting remark even if it's amusing. It doesn't look like making yourself rich at the expense of others.

Having considered what love is not, how can you tell if love is genuine? One way is to see if people give of themselves when it isn't easy, when it's not convenient and when loving another exacts a price.

Invest in love

Some think our mother's brand of nurturing love has no place in the business world. Martha Ann Walls, the president of Southern Newspapers thinks it's one of the most important investments one can make. She and her daughter Lissa Walls-Vahldiek, the company's chief operating officer, run their successful newspaper company with a combination of toughness, grace and, yes, love.

I first got to really know Mrs. Walls on a business trip. This one called for the toughness part. We were flying north in the company plane to fire a newspaper publisher for gross miss-management.

Tall, elegant and impeccably dressed, there was no question who was in charge when she marched into that newspaper office with her accountant and attorney to do the deed.

I was along to take over the newly vacated publisher's position. We went through the building and the books to discover an even bigger mess than we'd imagined. It would obviously take years to re-build all the damage to staff, the bank account, the news product, the building and the relationship with the community. Finally, after hours of work, the team was ready to leave me to the task ahead. Just as she was leaving for the airport, Mrs. Walls stopped.

As a teenager I was in a car wreck that landed me in the hospital. All would eventually heal but there were a few rough days. I'll never forget the look on my mother's face when she left me that first night—a look that poured out sorrow, empathy, love and concern.

Seventeen years later I saw the same look on Mrs. Walls' face. In an unpremeditated act of tenderness she reached out and touched my cheek. She held that pose for a moment and didn't say a word, but it was more than enough to tell me how sorry she was to leave me with such a daunting assignment. Her eyes were glistening as were mine when she turned and left.

At that moment, I would have crawled through a valley of broken glass for her.

Both Mrs. Walls and Lissa combined toughness and compassion to nurture those who worked for them. Neither would hesitate to challenge their publishers on issues of fair reporting or finance. Understated and never effusive, they could also make your day with a hand written note or by ending a long telephone conversation with a "thanks, dear." Annually they'd dip into corporate coffers to fully fund a three day meeting at a beautiful location for their publishers and their spouses. Light on meetings and long on pampering they made it clear the event was as much a thank you to their executives' spouses as it was the executives themselves. They cared about those who worked for them and it showed.

I talked with Mrs. Walls not long ago. A mutual friend was going through a difficult situation and we were comparing notes on how to help him. Well past the age most retire yet ever the executive, she discussed the issue in her usual matter-of-fact style. Then, just before we hung up, she said, "Come back to Houston and visit us. I could use a hug."

Is it any wonder talented people spent their entire careers happily working for women who understood nurturing and good business go hand in hand?

Love takes time

We are a busy people, and often that's good, because we enjoy many opportunities. We are able to fill our lives with fun, interesting, and important activities.

But the information revolution has brought us to a new level of busyness. Advertisers and bloggers on the Internet measure their success by how many "hits" they get, in other words by how many people read their message. But it also works the other way around.

If you're plugged into the latest technologically, you're subject to getting "hit" all the time, in all kinds of different ways. You can get hit 24 hours a day with sound, video and text from a rapidly expanding array of devices. It can be addicting and can rob time from deeper relationships.

One of my students recently complained in a writing assignment that his fiancée was addicted to checking her Blackberry. The pending argument was about whether or not she'd continue to do so during the honeymoon.

What his fiancée doesn't really understand is she's telling him that fooling with that tiny device is more important than paying attention to her husband to be.

Our mother would never have shown her love by sending a quick text-style message that read, "hw r u?" She'd look the person in the eyes and ask "How are you?" Then she'd listen with all her attention for as much time as it took.

One of the great time robbers is still television. The average U.S. family has the TV on eight hours a day.

One cultural analyst writes: "The infatuation and dependence on media activities has rapidly grown to steal time from other human activities, like face-to-face conversations . . . This subtle erosion is dangerous and difficult to detect. The media-techno driven world is having profound effects on every area of our lives. It has been said that our behaviors reveal what is in the heart of a man or woman. What do the behaviors of the American people tell us?" [2]

In all our relationships, we keep coming up against the issue of time. You cannot know another person unless you spend time with them.

And it has to be quality time. It doesn't mean every relationship has to be based on continual dialogue. Especially in long-term relationships, with people you spend years being close to, spells of companionable silence can be as deeply satisfying as conversation. But when you're building a relationship, time spent with the other person needs to be intentional, focused, interactive. We get to know the people we love better the more intentional time we spend with them.

Love when times are tough

Real love means being there for your family or friends even when it's really hard to do. That's particularly true in marriage. The best marriages bear witness to the surpassing beauty of mature love. Not gushy, sentimental love, not the love of glib phrases and easy promise, but love based on wisdom, built of experience, developed over time against all obstacles, burned into the fabric of human hearts.

With the power of love, our parents carved a life out of a marriage that started in the Depression when the real family issue wasn't whether or not they could afford a big-screen TV but rather if they'd have enough to eat. They built the foundations of their love by being there for each other through her dozen surgeries and multiple miscarriages and his operation that gave him a fifty percent chance of being paralyzed. They lived through three tornadoes, several car wrecks and the loss of a family business that left them financially destitute at an age when most people are thinking about retirement. To make ends meet, he went to work selling cars, and his proud, self-educated wife worked in the kitchen at the county hospital before she could find a position in a legal office.

They loved even when the other wasn't very loveable. They had fights and anger and pain. Sometimes loving was the hardest thing in the world particularly when there were so many troubles and their spouse was tough to be around, but they never, ever gave up on their love of each other.

It was no longer about the fireworks of first romance but rather the tenderness and tenacity that goes with spending day after day, year after year in the bleak confines of a nursing home while watching the love of your life slowly drift away.

Yet they loved each other. Sometimes they felt like giving up. But they didn't, and through all the years, they built something together that was lasting and a testimony to others.

Mother died ten days before their sixty-sixth wedding anniversary. And in all those years together, our parents modeled for us and for their wide community of family and friends the power of married love.

Love the unloveable

If we're going to increase our capacity to love and therefore expand the richness of our lives, we must learn to reach beyond ourselves and love the unlovable.

One night, our family was driving to what promised to be a highly contentious church meeting. It was based on one of those small-town controversies that makes enemies out of neighbors and destroys long-standing friendships.

In preparation for that meeting, our mother was earnestly reciting over and over again, "I will love my neighbor, I will love my neighbor, I will love my neighbor." With that mantra on her lips, she and Dad walked into the sanctuary.

The meeting was a bad one. Tempers flared; people shouted angry words. Though she was a strong woman who voiced her own opinion, our mother never lost sight of her real task throughout the meeting. In the crucial days that followed, she plied her commitment to love as a gentle balm to fresh wounds. Always failing to rise to any harsh words, she dropped off a freshly baked pie here, an invitation to coffee there, maybe an offer to watch their children after church next Sunday. As a result of working hard to love others while they were being the least loveable, she avoided losing some lifelong friends.

Sometimes you and I may have the opportunity to love someone unlovable. Certainly we all have plenty of opportunities to love when it's hard to, when there's absolutely nothing in it for you.

Love pays you back

In the book "Try Giving Yourself Away," author David Dunn has a message that seems easy, almost simplistic. He encourages us to reach out by helping and lifting up not only the people dear to us, but also total strangers—as the Good Samaritan did in the Bible story. [3]

Dunn writes: "Whenever the world grows a bit dull, or I feel low in spirit, I know at once what the trouble is: I have stopped trying to give myself away. Instinctively, I look around for some opportunity to share a bit of myself. It seldom takes long to find one. Then I begin to feel alive—to glow with a current of happiness.

"It is as though each of us were an electric bulb, some of low wattage, some high, but all of us are free to draw a supply of happiness from the world's inexhaustible current. And all of us are potential disseminators of light and warmth."

We're not saying you're supposed to throw yourself under a truck for other people or give your life away to such an extent that you rob the people closest to you or ruin your health or never have fun or find time to enjoy the things that renew and restore you. What Dunn is saying is that when we give ourselves to help another person—especially when it costs us something—we will be rewarded by an inner glow that comes to us in no other way.

Giving ourselves away in loving other people has rewards beyond the obvious ones of feeling good that we've helped someone meet their needs or solve a problem. Our health as individuals, our health—maybe even our survival—as a species may well depend on the power of love, intimacy and relationships.

The how-to of love is going to be different for each of us. A relationship is a living thing, and every relationship is different because each one of us is different. Yet when it comes to the practice of love, certain principles always apply:

Invest yourself in love.

Love takes time.

Love even when it's hard to do.

Love pays you back.

Practice love. It's worth the effort. The benefits are incalculable.

The good news is that it's never too late to begin. Never too late to open our minds and hearts to love. Never too late to accept, forgive, ask forgiveness, reach out—give time, support—make ourselves available to a friend or family member who needs us—act in kindness when our first inclination might be otherwise.

At whatever age and stage of our lives we are in, kindness, forgiveness and love are still the best gifts we can give other people—and ourselves.

Pay love forward

The premise of the movie "Pay it Forward" is to perform acts of love and kindness not necessarily expecting people to return your kindness—at least not to you directly. But the payback comes when others turn around and love someone else—in other words, they pay the love and acts of service forward.

Our mother loved not because she expected something in return, although plenty of people flocked to her and loved her back. But years later, her love has been "paid forward"—by her sons, by people like Barb Martin and others who were transformed by her care and concern.

Our mother was that perennially-shining light bulb that Dunn describes. She glowed with the radiance of love.

She treated every person she knew and met with equal courtesy, charity, compassion and respect. She looked for, and found, the best in all of us who came within the radar pattern of her love. But though Mom loved widely and deeply, she did not love foolishly. She adored her sons, but she didn't idolize us. We were expected to be good, moral, hard-working, polite and persistent.

"If there's anything I can't stand, it's a quitter," she'd say, her blue eyes trained on us with such ferocity there was no way we'd consider such an ignoble action.

She was the center of a web of love that held many in its grip. A thousand acts of kindness, large and small, made up the fabric of her life. When we were in high school and college, it was our parents who hosted parties, our mother to whom kids flocked for love, admonishment, acceptance, wisdom and surrogate parenting. For our mother, religion is best expressed in how you treat others.

And when we were launched into the world and began free-falling through the agonies of early adult challenges and mistakes, it was on the firm foundation of our mother's love and moral training and religious faith that we finally landed.

"Always remember," she would say, "God loves you, and He will take care of you."

These weren't just platitudes to her. She was orphaned at the age of two. The promise of a college education was wiped out by the Great Depression. She fought ill health her last twenty years.

To the end of her days, living in a nursing home and no longer able to speak, she greeted her health care workers with the sweet and brilliant smile that had not changed in all the years. And as they were met by that smile and the gentle, loving, patient nature that had become our mother in old age, they, too, were drawn into her circle of love.

Our mother had discovered the secret to happiness: give yourself away so others, too, can "pay it forward."

Teresa Grim wasn't crying, but from the long pauses between sentences, I could tell she was close to it. Still she chattered on during our phone conversation as she talked about the person who had changed her life.

"I got back my independence and my self-esteem because of her confidence in me," she said.

Teresa had been left rudderless after the breakup of a nine-year marriage. Friends and family finally talked her into going back to finish her college education, and during her first year, she got a part-time job at a local laboratory. There she met a new mentor who began to push her to do new things.

"She was so loving, so supportive and understanding. She never held a grudge, but she always pushed me when I needed it."

That was five years ago. When Teresa and I talked, she had been promoted three times and was a working microbiologist who sometimes traveled worldwide to teach and to train. Obviously happy with her life, she had remarried, was working on her master's degree and was expecting her first child.

"If I hadn't met Barb Martin, I wouldn't be here," she said. "I only hope I can live up to her example."

As Teresa said those words, somewhere our mother was smiling.

Questions for discussion:

- Think of three specific acts of love or service others have done for you—be it a word of encouragement, a favor or something someone has gone out of their way to do.
- Think of ways you could "pay it forward" to someone else.

For more about love:

- From the Nicholas Sparks book "The Notebook" and movie by the same name, what do you learn about the power of married love?
- Watch the movie "Gifted Hands, The Ben Carson Story," a 2009 TNT made-for-TV movie, or read the book by the same name. What effect did a mother's love have on the protagonist?

CHAPTER 10

The Power of Faith

"If you don't have faith,
I don't know where virtue comes from."
—Tony Dungy, retired NFL coach

Tom Sawyer as an old man didn't look like his creator, Mark Twain. He looked like our Uncle Howard.

He was our mother's uncle, and that made him our great-uncle. But we all called him Uncle, and he served as a surrogate grandfather on our mother's side of the family. His brush of silvery hair still bore traces of his boyish carrot top. His ears stuck out at a funny angle. His grin was crooked, impish and irresistible. His blue eyes darted and danced with mischief. Even his ambling gait made you want to follow him, you were sure, on some delightful misadventure. His stories, mostly about his prank-filled youth, were hilarious. We knew he was one of the most successful farmers in the county. But he seemed like a naughty boy misplaced in an old man's body. What we didn't know, until many years later, was that Uncle Howard's life had not been all fun and laughter and good times. He had once experienced great misfortune.

Shortly after he and our Aunt Lucy were married, they put every dollar they could save and borrow into buying a farm. Then catastrophe hit.

Long before the stock market crash of 1929, the Great Depression ground its heel into the farm belt. Banks failed. It would become a disaster of epic proportions.

The bank, which in good times had loaned Uncle Howard money on lenient terms, found itself on the verge of closing. Uncle Howard had no money to pay the mortgage. The bank foreclosed. Uncle Howard and Aunt Lucy lost more than their land and their home. They lost everything but their clothing and their household furnishings. The bank took their livestock and farm machinery in lieu of cash for back mortgage payments.

At forty years old with a wife and two small sons, Uncle Howard had to start over. What did he do? He wept, but he didn't whine. He and Aunt Lucy went to church and prayed to God for help. They found a farm to rent, with part of the crop as payment. They worked from dawn until after dusk, year after year. And they continued to put their faith in God. With the Second World War, farm prices sky-rocketed. They saved everything they could. Finally, they were able to buy another farm. They became prosperous, even wealthy. In one of his few solemn moments, Uncle Howard once said: "Our faith brought us through. Without God, we would not have survived."

It was faith in God that brought not only Uncle Howard and Aunt Lucy through the Depression but also many others we knew who had been similarly devastated.

Their generation was made up of remarkable people. Picture them in church, old as we remember them. The women are erect and dignified in their navy, gray or black dresses; white shoes in summer, black in winter, with their hair primly set in a neat bun; their only nod to cosmetics a touch of face powder. The men are broad-shouldered and lean, awkward in their once-weekly suit and tie and stiffly-starched white shirts. Their faces are lined and battered by years of exposure to sun and wind and heat and bitter cold. They sit with their big hands on their knees—hands gnarled and scarred and enlarged by lives of manual labor, tending livestock, tilling the land, feeding America.

Seeing them there, practicing the faith that had brought them through heartache, failure and disaster, the same faith that had also helped them forge successful new beginnings, you sense that somehow in their simplicity and lack of sophistication they were in touch with something deeper, more profound, more relevant to the living of life—in good times and bad—than most of the world knew.

These words from the Bible could describe their approach to life: "The fundamental fact of existence is that this trust in God, this faith, is the firm foundation under everything that makes life worth living. It's our handle on what we can't see. The act of faith is what distinguished our ancestors, set them above the crowd." (Hebrews 11:1, The Message.)

Faith delivers

When I was in my early thirties and long before I came to the ministry, I did what from this vantage point seems like a pretty foolhardy thing. I decided to buy a boat and teach myself to sail. I lived in Atlanta at the time, and there's an enormous man-made lake, Sidney Lanier, located about an hour's drive from the city.

With more hope than sense, I began. One of the first times I went out on my new boat was an autumn Saturday that started out bright and sunny. I took along a friend who knew only slightly more about sailing than I. We ran up the sails and had achieved a creditable reach when calamity hit. Fog—one of the worst fogs I've ever seen—came out of nowhere. The wind died with it. We got the sails down, turned on the engine and then realized we could go nowhere. We literally could not see beyond the rails of the boat. Added to the fear that we might run into another boat or crash into shore came the gathering realization that we were lost in the middle of a huge lake with no end to the fog in sight and, in those pre-cell-phone days, no way of calling for help.

So we sat, hearing the occasional honking of horns from boats around the lake signaling their placement to hopefully avoid being run into. One hour passed, then two. Our frustration and anxiety mounted.

I didn't realize it then, but being lost in the fog on my boat on Lake Lanier that day many years ago was a metaphor for where I was in my life at the time. I had moved to Atlanta in the fall of 1974 to take the job of director of corporate communications for a large commercial real estate company, Crow, Carter and Associates.

Within months, my world fell apart. Emotional problems I'd been living on top of since late adolescence surfaced to torment me on a daily basis. The word torment is not an understatement. I was obsessed by anxious thoughts. I could mostly function on the job and with other people, but internally, I was an emotional battleground. I was convinced something terrible was about to happen to me. Imagined enemies plagued me. I could not separate fact from fiction. I was losing control of my mind.

I'd battled these awful fear thoughts for years. I'd tried therapy, medication, drinking too much alcohol, Eastern religion and astrology to ease the mental anguish. Nothing helped. Then at the chance invitation of a new friend, I began attending a large church not far from where I lived. The church offered prayer groups on weekday evenings where small groups of the larger congregation could convene for more intimate fellowship. The weekly format was simple: we'd gather for some informal singing, a little Bible reading. Sometimes a member of the group would give a brief, faith-based teaching. Then we'd end by praying for each other.

After I'd been a part of the group long enough to feel safe, I finally admitted that I, too, had a prayer request. I told them of the anguish that had driven me to the edge of despair. Two older women came and laid hands on me and began to pray. They prayed that I would be delivered from the suffering that had made my life hell for so long. And that night I was set free.

Thirty-five years have passed since that night, and I've never experienced a return of the tormenting thoughts. What that proves to me is that God is a living presence and that He's here to help you, as He helped me, to find victory over your life-dominating problems.

Two fog-bound hours became three that day on Lake Lanier. Then, so suddenly and unexpectedly I thought it might be some kind of hallucination, I heard a man's voice beside our boat.

He said, "We're right beside you. Are you all right?"

I said, "We're okay, but how are we going to get out of here?"

He said, "Follow me."

I said, "What do you mean follow you? I can't even see you."

The stranger said, "I have equipment. I'll ring a bell. Follow the bell."

It was a gentle, silvery sound—the bell that led us through the fog to shore and a safe mooring that day. Just as we reached land, the fog lifted. The sun came out. We could see clearly. Choked up with the emotion of relief, we put the boat to rights, jumped into the car and headed home.

Faith is simple

Look around you at today's world and you see the problems that persist and that, in one way or another, affect us all. Illness. Starvation. Economic crisis. Crime. War. Global warming. Lack of health care. Immorality.

Our world suffers in each of these areas. But at the core of all our problems, as individuals and as nations, lies an even greater need—the need for faith, a faith so authentic that it informs and transforms every area of existence.

What all people need is a faith so strong it becomes their stabilizing force; an inner resource they can always depend on; a power that helps bring them through adversity not shattered but intact and enables them to emerge as whole persons.

We're Christians. Our faith is in the triune God—God the Father, God the Son, God the Holy Spirit—as presented in the Old and New Testaments. Our purpose in writing this book is not to convert you to Christianity—it's to encourage you to develop and deepen an existing faith or, if you are not a person of faith, to become one.

Faith varies for all of us, just as our image and understanding of God is different.

For example, the Twelve Step programs, which began with Alcoholics Anonymous and have expanded to include programs designed to help people cope with everything from additions to drugs, gambling, and even sex, foster belief in what they call a Higher Power and "the God of your understanding." We were all designed to need some power beyond ourselves, some power greater than our own, to help us through life.

Faith doesn't have to be complicated. Our parents, the generation that followed Uncle Howard's, also were damaged by the Depression. But they never let themselves become victims of it.

In the early 1930s, the bank that held our mother's trust fund folded, ending her chance for a college education. Our father's family never even considered college for any of their children. Both our parents worked as teenagers at back-breaking jobs. Mom picked vegetables for the local canning factory. Dad worked first as a farm laborer, later as a truck driver.

Dad said, "Your mother and I thought we'd wait to get married until we could afford it. Finally, since we decided we'd never be able to afford it, we got married anyway."

After the wedding, Dad gave the minister, Mom's cousin Kenneth, $10 for performing the ceremony. Kenneth gave it back to Dad, as his wedding gift.

Dad said, "It was wonderful! On that $10, we were able to eat for a week!"

Our parents, like the rest of their family and many of their friends who were similarly devastated by the Depression, endured the tough times and survived them because they had what our mother called gumption—enterprise, initiative and common sense. Gumption was the quality possessed by Mom's fictional predecessor Scarlett O'Hara in "Gone With the Wind." Gumption was the quality Scarlett's creator, Margaret Mitchell, said was the reason Scarlett was able to survive the twin catastrophes of the Civil War and Reconstruction.

The worst thing our mother could say about another person was that they had no gumption.

Mom and all her family had gumption to a marked degree. The other thing they had in common, their even more crucial survival tool, was their faith. They survived because they built the platform of their lives on a God they trusted to give them the power to endure any adversity and emerge victorious. When asked what faith meant to her, our mother said: "It means God will take care of you."

Faith carries you

Not long ago, I attended a conference of Episcopal clergy. Clergy new to our diocese stood and introduced themselves. The last to do so stood in the back. I couldn't see, but could only hear a familiar voice identifying himself as Budu Shannon.

I hadn't seen Budu in many years, since he and I graduated together from Virginia Theological Seminary in Alexandria. After the meeting, Budu and I greeted each other and he began pouring out some of what had happened to him in the years since seminary. He is a native of Liberia. After seminary, he'd returned home to pastor a local Anglican parish. Then came a guerilla-led insurrection against the Liberian establishment, of which the Anglican Church was a part.

Budu was arrested and tied to a tree while his house and the homes around him were burned. People were murdered before his eyes.

Budu was stripped. Everything was taken from him—home, ministry, respect, the support of a just government. Finally, he was set free—with only his life. But he survived to answer a call to ministry in the United States.

Budu said, "I was stripped of everything . . . but God." He paused, then added, "but that was enough."

That's the lesson Budu Shannon learned through his time of testing. It's the lesson God has for you, too.

Faith and success

In January 2007, Tony Dungy became the first African-American coach in the history of the National Football League to win a Super Bowl. It was a remarkable event for two reasons. First, it was the first Super Bowl to have not one, but two African-American coaches. The Chicago Bears and their coach, Lovie Smith—also Dungy's good friend—were on the opposite side of the field that day. And it was remarkable because both Dungy and Smith for years had been publicly open about their faith, a faith that they ultimately credited as the foundation for their success as coaches.

Dungy said in an interview on the field after the game, "More than anything, I've said it before, Lovie Smith and I, are not only the first two African-Americans, but Christian coaches showing that you can win doing it the Lord's way. And we're more proud of that." [1]

Faith gives purpose

Many people discover faith through crisis, but faith is more than just a salve in hard times. It's a way of life that can give you a sense of purpose, and hard times become the platform from which that purpose grows.

When Lisa Gibson from Colorado Springs, Colorado, was a freshman in college, her older brother, Ken, was killed in the terrorist bombing of Pan Am Flight 103 over Lockerbie, Scotland. All 259 people on board were killed in the December 1988 attack, along with eleven people on the ground. Since 180 victims were Americans, the Lockerbie bombing was the deadliest terrorist attack on American citizens until Sept. 11, 2001.

A Libyan intelligence agent was convicted in connection with the bombing, and the country of Libya ultimately took responsibility for the incident and agreed to pay restitution to the victim's families.

It's easy to blame God and blame others when tragedy strikes. Gibson wouldn't settle for either. On the contrary, she found herself challenged to live out her Christian faith, which taught her to love her enemies.

She wrote a book about her experience: "Life in Death: Journey from Terrorism to Triumph." In it, she wrote, "As a believer, I knew it was wrong to hate . . . For years I resolved myself to being indifferent to Muslims.

"But then God began to challenge me on what His word says about loving my enemies . . . I was confronted with the reality that, as a follower of Christ, I was expected to behave in a way that was different than everyone else. It was counter-cultural . . . Many of the Lockerbie family members were crippled with anger and bitterness toward Libyans.

"It was not enough for me to just not hate Libyans or Muslims. I was called to love Muslims." [2]

In January 2005, Gibson was among the first Americans to visit Libya in nearly two decades after the U.S. imposed sanctions on the north African nation following the Lockerbie bombing. She told her story to ordinary Libyans and government officials alike.

"Some feared that my reasons for coming were to cause trouble . . . As I assured them of my good intentions of being in Libya, people became more at ease . . . as I shared my story, time and again I would see the walls fall. Even grown Libyan men began to weep. One of our guides . . . took me into his arms and said, 'It is so good for you to come. I will do anything I can to help you.'" [3]

Gibson has since started a nonprofit organization called the Peace and Prosperity Alliance, which builds bridges of friendship between leaders of the developed and the developing world through education, training and humanitarian assistance. Most of the organization's efforts are focused on Libya, the very country that took responsibility for the death of Gibson's brother.

Through faith, Gibson has found purpose for her loss.

"Taking hate and turning it around with love is the only way to make my brother's death not be in vain," she said. [4]

Faith builds a place of belonging

We've moved a lot. Since graduating from college, between the two of us, we've lived in eleven states. In this, we are not unlike many who move or are transferred by job necessities in the search of the American Dream. All these moves can be jarring, disturbing and stressful on families. In every move, it has been through joining a church that we've found a sense of belonging, a renewed sense of who we are as people. In many congregations, we've even found surrogate family members who make up a little for our living so far from our family of origin.

And all these new communities have reminded us of how much strength, both spiritual and emotional, we've derived through the years from being rooted in the hometown, prairie church of our youth.

Our little church was the only one in a village perched on the edge of rolling farmland. Life was admittedly simpler in rural middle-America in the 1950s and 60s. But life was also vibrant for us, rich with activities, enthusiasm, hard work and profound commitment to values and a way of life that seems to be slipping away. Home, school and church—these were our centers.

People gather in places of worship for a variety of reasons, be it habit, purpose, service, comfort or support. Families may, as we have done, move all over the country or even around the world, but come to your religious community and you find continuity, a place where you will always belong.

Our religious traditions affirm who God is for us, that we are His people, that He has a plan for us and guidance for how we may best live our lives.

Take away our traditions and you take away our identity.

When we were boys growing up, we didn't miss church—except when we were sick or on vacation. It if was Sunday, we went to church.

And what did we have to show for all this church attendance, except for a lot of great memories and a dangling chain of Sunday school attendance awards? What did we have to show for the discipline, the dedication, the determination, the dogged devotion to God and the little prairie church? Were we better people for it? Perhaps, although for us, in some ways, goodness was a bit late in coming. But if we were not better people, we were different people. Seeds of faith were planted. In all those years of showing up, listening to the lessons and sermons, singing the old hymns and doing the work we were given to do, the imprint of the living God was etched in our hearts. That has been a reality for us ever since and a source of strength, courage and hope for the living of our lives.

Faith gives you gumption

Take another look around our little church on a typical Sunday morning and you see, along with Uncle Howard and Aunt Lucy and their contemporaries, survivors of a younger generation.

You see Polly Lindquist, red-haired, irrepressible, wearing as she always did her expression of hopeful expectation, even though she'd soon leave church and go home to the bedridden husband for whom she was the sole caregiver, while she also raised their two children. See always fun, always enterprising Marie Van Metre, up front directing the choir. Orphaned as an infant and left with no family, she'd been taken in by neighbors, and now she's taken in their elderly, unmarried, often crotchety daughter to live with her husband and children.

See Eunice Tucker, who'd married much-older Frank thinking, as the town gossips said, that he had money, only to find that not only was he broke he was going blind. Eunice survived and kept Frank and herself going, first by taking in boarders and then by baking angel food cakes that were famous throughout the county. See Roger Sparks, with his legs lost in the war, he has hobbled to church on his poorly-made prosthetics, as he hobbles his way through life, doing the work of three men as a farmer, raising a family and never forgetting to laugh. See lovely and serene Garnet Griffiths. Who would guess that she, too, had been devastated as a young woman by the Depression? See our parents, faithful to the core, who by gumption, humor, persistence and faith, refuse to be defeated.

Nearly every person in our church had suffered crushing misfortunes, yet each had survived and thrived because they had faith. So can you.

Questions for discussion:

- How do you define faith? What do you have faith in?
- If you're not a person of faith, find someone who is, buy them a cup of coffee and ask them about it.
- Describe how faith has impacted you or someone you know.

For more about faith:

- Watch the movie "Amazing Grace," and see how that story relates to the power of faith.
- Read Dr. Koenig's book, "The Healing Power of Faith: How Belief and Prayer Can Help You Triumph Over Disease."

CHAPTER 11

The Power of Dignity

"I've known people that the world has thrown everything
at to discourage them, to kill them, to break their spirit.
And yet something about them retains a dignity."
—Horton Foote

Horton Foote, the Oscar and Pulitzer-prize winning playwright, might have been describing our father's mother, our Grandmother Elsberry.

Grandma was born in 1888, the granddaughter of pioneers. Before she died, she held her great-grandchildren in her arms. Like the fine wire the first settlers used to fence in their livestock, Grandma Elsberry held generations of our family together with grace, love and dignity.

Our grandmother's life was hard and full of deprivation but all my memories of her have to do with abundance.

I'm there in the upstairs bedroom of my grandparents' old farmhouse. It's early morning. The rooster is crowing outside, the fragrance of my grandmother's freshly-baked bread permeates the house, and my grandfather, in from milking, is calling me to breakfast. I come down to the unique smell of Grandma's kitchen, the fresh bread fragrance mixed with the scent of wood burning in the old cook stove and the soap she used to rigorously scrub the cracked linoleum. The smell of comfort.

I can be in a stressful situation today, and the memory of that unique fragrance still has the power to ground and soothe me. In wintertime, she added the arresting odor of hyacinths blooming from bulbs forced in her kitchen windows. The strong scent and gaudy blossoms were a defiant reminder that if one would simply endure the winter with its snow drifts banked to the window sills, spring would come.

She knew a great deal of enduring. Her life had not turned out as she hoped. She was sensitive, creative and artistic. She loved books, music and flowers. With her poise and graciousness, she could have been a fine lady who spent her days entertaining or painting. Instead, she married our grandfather, an adventurer who took her into what in the early 1900s was the frontier of northern Wisconsin. Land was cheap. He saw an opportunity to carve a new beginning for his family out of the great north woods. Like the earlier pioneers, our grandparents started over—clearing the land of trees and stones, building house and farm buildings by hand, enduring winters even colder and with more snow than they'd left behind in Iowa. They also endured isolation beyond anything they'd imagined.

They were resourceful and hard-working, but the promise failed. The land was too poor to support crops for more than a few years. For our grandmother, thrust into a harsh, alien environment far from family and friends, the loneliness must have been at times unbearable.

Life was nonstop work, childbearing and childrearing a family of eight. She grew the food they ate, canned it, cooked it and served it in an endless litany of service to her family.

There seemed to always be an abundance of food. As a toddler, I remember her keeping me close with the gentle tether of her attention as she conjured up meals of seemingly endless dishes with apparently little effort. All her food was simple but wonderful, centered on produce she'd grown, harvested and stored. I marveled at her Aladdin's Cave of gleaming jars of vegetables stored on tall shelves in the root cellar. In summer, all the vegetables were fresh, a panoply of bounty you had to experience to imagine: Bushel baskets brimming with Concord grapes she'd picked from the arbor that foretold jars of jams and jellies. Succulent tomatoes and beans from her huge, carefully ordered garden. Strawberries from the patch out by the back fence. Breakfast eggs from Grandma's prize Road Island Red hens that boasted firm orange-colored yolks. As I child, I reveled in all of these treasures without ever once considering the non-stop labor they demanded. Grandma never complained or even appeared to be working that hard. She just seemed to always be pleasantly busy.

They returned from Wisconsin in time for the Depression that hit the heartland before it hit Wall Street. Our grandparents and their younger children moved in with our great-grandparents. Grandma cared for both of them, and for her own mother, in their old age. From dawn until bedtime, she was on her feet: gardening, cooking, cleaning, washing, mending, caring—always caring—for others.

I had the flu. Bundled up on Grandma's living room couch, I could hear her bustle around the house. Grandma never stood still, but she seemed to carry stillness with her. At my smallest complaint, she was at my side, cool hands on my forehead, warm tea or chicken broth for my itchy throat. In my heart of hearts, I had to admit I rather liked being sick at Grandma's house.

Then tragedy hit. Their sixteen-year-old son John, Jr., died of cancer. Only someone who has lost a child can possibly comprehend the devastation our grandparents experienced. Yet our grandmother retained her dignity, a combination of reserve, discretion and stoicism. In today's world of reality TV, of morning shows that feature tearful interviews with those who've suffered the tragedy of the day, in our "How do you feel?" culture, it's hard to imagine Grandma's refusal to bleed her grief on others. Conceivably, she would have been better off had she been able to find therapeutic support to help her work through her loss. But therapy was not affordable. Nor was it the norm. So she swallowed her grief and did what she always had—she simply carried on.

Best of all, was dusk. Then Grandma would bring out the kerosene lanterns, trim the wicks, light them and set them around the house. The lighting was mysterious, evocative of the old days on the prairie and reminiscent of simpler times. Evening descended like a benediction. With Grandma's arms around me as we read a book or the Bible, in the old house built by her grandfather the pioneer, peace reigned.

Finally, in her later years, the rheumatoid arthritis that she had kept at bay with her constant motion finally won the battle for her body. Knees perpetually drawn up and clenched, fingers turned back on themselves in impossible arcs, she couldn't leave the bed Grandpa had set up in the drawing room.

Full of myself as a fast-growing teenager, I'd go to Grandma's beside. She always seemed so interested in my adolescent triumphs and agonies. I'd jabber on for hours, and she'd listen intently all the while dispensing the same quiet love and wisdom that she always had.

It was only much later that I came to understand some of the agonies of my grandmother's life. The regal, gentle woman I'd loved and who had loved me, had endured a life of crippling labor, personal loss and financial ruin. Composed and loving to the end or her days, I never heard her complain or yell or cry. Only in adulthood did I realize the despair that she conquered with quiet determination and dignity, and then, finally, I shed the tears she never had.

Dignity is about respect

Dignity is innate. It can be based on self-confidence. But dignity and self-confidence are not the same. Sadly, plenty of self-confident people go through life and never exhibit a trace of dignity. Nor is dignity the same thing as integrity, although the two often co-exist.

You have to experience dignity in a person to understand its power. You have to see real dignity in action. Not the façade of dignity but dignity that issues from deep within a person's character and personality.

Dignity is obvious

We don't talk about dignity much anymore. To some it conjures up images of stuffy old Colonels or doctors in old "Murder She Wrote" re-runs. You know the type: formal, outdated clothes, pompous bearing, and English accent. To many people, dignity is a joke.

Not to us. To us dignity is about respect. It's about respecting yourself and those around you. People with dignity carry themselves with a quiet self-confidence that doesn't need reinforcement of braying self-promotion. They treat everyone they meet—everyone—with the same respect.

Growing up, we were surrounded by so much dignity that it was a shock when we entered a larger world that had its share of the selfish and self-centered with their endless self-aggrandizing and temper tantrums. These people were very different from our role models.

People with dignity come in all ages, sizes and occupations. Perhaps the janitor at your work has it, while maybe the person in the corner office doesn't.

Dignity withstands crisis

It's not all that difficult to have dignity under normal circumstances. The real test comes in crisis. The Bustillos family of Weld County, Colorado, is a perfect example. On a fall afternoon, 17-year-old Tania Bustillos was driving home with family members Miguel, 12, Enrique, 15, and 3-month-old Destiny. Apparently distracted, she ran a stop sign and broadsided a Ford pickup. Before the week ended, Miguel, Enrique and Destiny had died and Tania was still in intensive care. [1]

Only those who've lived through such tragedy can imagine the horror and grief Grasiela and Valentin Bustillos experienced over the losses of those children.

Imagine how they felt when a politician from 150 miles away decided to turn the incident into a campaign issue. He was running for a state senate seat in an impending election and sent an e-mail to the local newspaper.

"Was the driver properly licensed?" he asked in the e-mail. "Was the vehicle properly registered and insured? Why aren't these facts part of your published article? Was this person the child of parents in the U.S. illegally? Or was she here illegally?"

He then railed on to his campaign speech; "I am extremely concerned with the dramatic rise in crime caused by those illegally in this country over the past 10-15 years or so. Why is it that the investigative reports we read in the papers and see on TV do not point out the fact that these accidents and the resulting cost to taxpayers (hospitalization, etc.) are a direct result of our lax immigration policies and enforcement?"

His pandering to a "get tough on immigration" plank in his campaign platform suddenly threw the Bustillos family into the middle of a media storm. Never mind the thoughtless insensitivity of a person more interested in votes than simple compassion. Reporters from all over the region began to hound the family for their reaction. Members of both political parties clamored for the spotlight as they tried to turn the situation to their advantage.

Who can say how they'd respond if thrust into the same situation? A family could be forgiven for bouts of rage and some level of retaliation. Certainly many of the righteously indignant, and those willing to pose as such to further their own ends, were ready to help them mount a scathing counterattack.

Here, instead, is what the Bustillos did:

They refused to talk to the outside media.

The family donated their children's organs so other children could live.

Then they buried their family members and mourned for them.

They asked that all the financial donations that had poured in go directly to Children's Hospital in Denver, where two of the children died, or to North Colorado Medical Center in Greeley, where their daughter was still in intensive care. Despite being far from rich, they said they didn't want it for themselves but that they knew the hospitals needed it.

After all that was finished, they wrote a letter to the politician. In it they told him the car was properly registered and insured and that the driver had followed the required state of Colorado protocol to obtain a driving permit. They told him all the children involved in the accident were American citizens as was Tania's mother, Grasiela. They said her husband, Valentin, was a legal resident who had worked and paid taxes here for 12 years.

They said they were praying for him and ended with. "God bless you."

The Bustillos family taught an over-reaching politician and all who were watching about dignity under the worst of circumstances.

Dignity inspires

Dignity not only carries people through obstacles, often, it can make or break a career.

Unfortunately, not all managers understand that. In a Wall Street Journal column, Carol Hymowitz chronicled "screaming bully bosses" who yelled, threw things at employees and called them at all hours to inflict even more punishment. In that column, James Clifton, CEO of the Gallup Organization, was quoted as saying those sorts of managers "undermine productivity, discourage innovation" and may run off good talent. [2]

Of course they do. Who wants to be screamed at?

People respond to respect, not degradation. Sure, a screaming manager may reach a high level of authority, but the best and brightest, those who respect themselves, won't work for that sort of person for long.

I had the good fortune to work for a man who understood that. Phil Swift, founder of Swift Communications, started with nothing after he returned from service as a pilot during World War II. Ultimately, he built a media group worth millions of dollars by relying on his own natural dignity. Smart and insightful, he hired the best and brightest and managed them with respect. His biggest management tool didn't rely on invective, directive or volume. A small man of huge character, he often led by simply asking questions. Those who were successful in his organization knew they wouldn't be subjected to a long-distance rant in the middle of the night, but if Mr. Swift asked if they'd reviewed their expenses recently, they might pull an all-nighter to see what he'd found that they hadn't.

Those who didn't respond to such questions probably would end up working elsewhere. Managing with dignity and respect didn't mean Swift was unwilling to replace those who couldn't do the job. It did mean those who could do the job often happily worked for him for a very long time.

Dignity empowers

People with dignity share it without discrimination. There are those who respect and show kindness to the prestigious and powerful while gleefully ripping into any waitress or bellboy that crosses their path—but are those the kind of people you want to spend your time with?

In a Wall Street Journal story, Peter Wood, author of "A Bee in the Mouth: Anger in America Now," asserts that we have become "a culture that celebrates anger" and that "living in the United States has become a matter of dealing with angry people almost all the time—or at least a lot more frequently than we would like." [3]

Certainly it's easy to find angry people in the workplace, in the supermarket checkout line and most certainly on the roadways. Many television "talking heads" have now become "screaming heads," and heaven save us from the vituperative nonsense of talk radio. The best remedy for all this hot air is to keep your dignity—and your cool—when others lose theirs.

There must be a special place in heaven for the airline service agents who keep their temper in the face of a flight grounded for safety reasons while hordes of people scream their displeasure. Who do you respect more—the overbearing loudmouth who thinks by yelling louder the plane will be able to take off in an ice storm or the person across the counter who never loses her cool?

People with dignity laugh with people but never at them. They can be angry but never hateful or irrational. While they have a healthy sense of self, they're always aware of the needs of others. They admit when they've been wrong and let others figure out for themselves when they're right.

People with dignity are admired and respected, and they empower others to respect themselves. Start using the power of dignity, and you'll start changing lives, beginning with your own.

Questions for discussion:

- Was does dignity mean to you?
- Do you know someone of dignity who has what many would think of as a menial job?
- Have you ever known someone who mistreated those they thought were beneath them? How did that make you feel?
- Think of a time when you or someone you know lost their dignity. What could have been done to retain it in that situation?

For more on dignity:

- Watch the 1997 movie "Titanic." Decide for yourself which characters have dignity and which don't.

CHAPTER 12

The Power of Integrity

"If you have integrity, nothing else matters.
If you don't have integrity, nothing else matters."
—Senator Alan Simpson

It wasn't supposed to turn out this way. How could his business be failing? All those years spent building a clientele in the neighboring farm communities. He'd lived most of his life here and knew so many people who had bought cars from him. Then there was the slow climb from sales rookie to top salesman, sales manager and then, on one of the proudest moments of his life, the day he signed the papers to buy the dealership. He remembered how he felt when the crane dropped in the new sign "Elsberry Oldsmobile."

Sure he was at an age when others were talking about how to retire. Who cared? This was his chance, his moment, the opportunity of a lifetime. How could it have all gone so terribly wrong? He'd put up their life savings and borrowed heavily to make the deal work. But so what? He knew this business, and he knew how to make it thrive. How could he have known the economy would crash, taking farm prices with it, or that GM would go on strike and there wouldn't be enough cars to sell? Who would think so many people would want those new little Japanese rattle traps? He worked harder and harder, desperate to close more deals. But it wasn't enough.

He hated the look of worry in his wife's eyes. He hated the soul-crushing weight of dodging the calls from vendors, many longtime friends, with past-due bills. He hated watching all his dreams die such an ugly death. His son and daughter-in-law kept pushing him to take bankruptcy. They said it was an honorable way out, but how could he do that? He'd signed contracts, he'd made promises, and he had given his word.

Our father finally sold his car franchise at a great loss in 1972. He was 59. He went to work as a bottom-of-the-ladder car salesman for the new, multi-brand dealership and was the "top man" with the most cars sold in his first month. He worked sixty-hour weeks until age seventy-eight and was top man in his last month on the job. He never took bankruptcy, and in the intervening nineteen years, he settled every debt.

He taught the lesson of integrity the same way he had learned it from his father—by living it.

When you look at the fundamental parts of our boyhood community, love was its heart, faith was its soul, optimism its spirit and the solid rock of its character was integrity. It was an integrity built on everyday ethics taught by example. We lived in a town of people who believed that character and honesty were the measure of a man. They found that living a successful, happy life wasn't based on new toys and trinkets; it was based on living to a higher standard and doing the right thing.

Some of our neighbors were close to what today we'd call "subsistence farmers." They labored long hours in the fields, feedlots and milking parlors just to feed their families. But their families were fed and showed up for Sunday church in neatly washed and pressed clothes. Regardless of the family finances, they always placed an offering in the collection plate for the same reason they always paid their bills and took care of their own, because they had pledged to do so.

Many a man with a faded feed cap, worn bib overalls and dirty work boots could hold his head high in our town because people knew he was a man of his word. That phrase was more important than wealth or family connections. As children, we were reprimanded if we backed out on a promise. Our parents taught that when you gave your word, it meant something.

Integrity reclaimed

A few more people like them and we might have avoided the greatest global recession of our time. By now, we all know it started in the fall of 2008 with America's sub-prime mortgage mess and the total lack of integrity that spawned it. Two presidents pushed to open up home ownership to more people. Mortgage rates dropped, loan requirements were loosened and houses began to sell faster than they could be built. Millions of Americans rushed to jump on the bandwagon.

The genie was out of the bottle. Loan originators raked in hefty commissions to close loans, not to check if the applicant for the 100 percent mortgage could afford the payments. Banks got paid to rubber stamp those mortgages and pass them on to huge, and now defunct, investment firms like Bear Stearns and Lehman Brothers. They in turn packaged these high-risk mortgages into triple-A rated securities (blessed by the sleeping watch dogs at the federal rating agencies) and then sold them for big profits around the globe. Paste the whole thing together with the high-finance voodoo of "credit default swaps" to insure the whole thing and then have a party; we were all going to get rich.

And for a while, we did. Everyone in the tawdry supply chain made money. Middle-class Americans moved into the homes of their dreams, and when the values of those homes appreciated, they cashed in the difference with second mortgages that helped buy everything from new SUVs and Harleys to trips to the Caribbean. Top dogs on Wall Street blissfully handed each other multi-million dollar bonuses, and life was good.

Then the bills came due. Finally the real estate prices stalled and those with ballooning adjustable rate mortgages couldn't refinance. Others who had borrowed to the hilt on their home's appreciation found they couldn't make all those payments. They began to simply walk away from their creditors. The housing market cratered, billions of dollars in mortgage backed securities became worthless, world stock markets crashed and everyone knows about the economic carnage that followed.

There was plenty of shame to go around. It was easy to point fingers at the loan originators, bankers, investment houses and Wall Street big wigs. Some deserved it. Each sector proved to be more interested in making a fast buck than doing the right thing.

But that's not where it started. It started with the American consumer who, despite living in the most prosperous nation on earth, clambered for more. In spite of all the new-found wealth, our greed still pushed the national saving rate into negative numbers. Then when it came time to pay the piper, many simply walked away from the party.

Shame on us.

So how does a nation or an individual begin to reclaim lost integrity? When Oscar Wilde arrived for a visit to the United States in 1882, he was asked by Customs officials if he had anything to declare. He replied: "Only my genius." Fifteen years later, alone and in prison, he reflected on his life of waste and excess: "I have been a spendthrift of my genius. I forgot that every little action of the common day makes or unmakes character."[1]

Nothing can ever be done about the past. We reclaim integrity by what we do every day from this day forward.

Integrity is built one action at a time

Our friend and fellow Iowa boy Al Weber still tells the story of his first home run. "I was nine years old when I finally knocked one right out of our front yard—straight into the stained-glass window of the church across the street. I was terrified when I told my father what happened. He was very calm as he loaded me in the family station-wagon and drove me to the minister's home. When we got there, he said we needed to go tell the pastor what happened and to ask him how much it would cost to fix. Next, he suggested I start thinking about how I was going to pay for it. Then he really shocked me when he said, 'I'll wait here.' I'll never forget the lonely walk up to that door. It was one of the scariest things I've ever done."

Al's father, like ours and nearly every other adult we knew growing up, made sure we practiced everyday ethics on the small things, because they knew character was built one step at a time.

How do we find and use integrity? By discerning that some beliefs, some actions, are better than others. There is still right and wrong. Then by acting on those beliefs—even when it's unpopular, even when it costs us, even when it hurts.

Integrity isn't about popularity

Often standing up for what you believe in can make you decidedly unpopular. Take the story of Mike Slaughter, the small-town football coach who suspended 16 starters—one his own son—on the eve of the team's first trip to the Illinois state championship. [2] Those who follow community football will tell you that's the sort of thing that could cost a man his job, but Slaughter decided there were more important things at stake.

In an Associated Press story, he said it all came down to accountability. "It doesn't matter if they drank half a beer or a six-pack, they still broke the rules. I always told my boys that if you get in trouble with alcohol, tobacco, drugs, I will suspend you from the team." His team went on to lose sixty-five to nothing in the final but came away winners of a different sort.

As related in the story "At the end, the players took off their helmets and held them to the sky as they had in victory, then went charging up the stairs to the locker room as the crowd of 1,300 gave them a standing ovation." Slaughter said, "The applause, the remarks from people, it was overwhelming. These kids had tears in their eyes, partly because of what had gone on but also because of the positive attitude that we got from the Marquette community."

Slaughter had no idea how his town or team would react when he made his decision to bench the starters. He just knew it was the right thing to do, not only for the moment but for the life lessons his team would take with them into adulthood.

Integrity costs

Sometimes integrity is what you do when no one is watching. Take for example J.P. Hayes, who knowingly cost himself a six-figure income on the PGA circuit when he turned himself in for an inadvertently using the wrong golf ball. [3] It happened during the PGA Tour qualifying tournament. One night after the day's round, Hayes realized the ball he had played was a prototype that wasn't approved for PGA play. Knowing full well what it would mean, he called officials anyway. He was eventually disqualified from PGA competition for a year. The prior year, Hayes won more than $300,000 on the tour and had lifetime earnings of more than $7 million.

His response? "It was my mistake. I had no choice but to take my medicine." He owned up to his error and took the financial penalty.

Compare that to the Wall Street types who in 2008 absconded with huge golden parachutes before bailing out of the businesses they'd run into the ground and leaving the American taxpayers a multibillion dollar tab. The difference is called integrity.

I have the good fortune to teach at The Monfort College of Business at the University of Northern Colorado. It's a gem of a school and a winner of America's Malcolm Baldrige Award for quality. Graduates typically rank in the top five percent nationally on post-graduate exams. That kind of reputation attracts bright, sincere students. During the spring 2009 semester, a class was discussing coach Slaughter and J.P. Hayes when a student raised his hand. "Why is it a coach and a golfer give us examples of integrity but our business leaders don't?" he asked.

Good question. And why wouldn't he ask that? Despite the thousands of business people who worked at doing the right thing every day, you wouldn't know it from recent media coverage. The copies of the Wall Street Journal stacked outside the classrooms had been littered with one business scandal after another. From billionaire ripoff artist Bernie Madoff to the Wall Street elite who fiddled away multimillion dollar bonuses and million-dollar office remodels while their companies and the international economy burned, there hadn't been much to admire in American business.

The students know what integrity doesn't look like, and it shows up in their writing assignments: The bottling company that promotes recycling and secretly dumps bottles in the trash; the national chain that offers annual bonuses for mid-managers and lays them off just before those bonuses get paid; the stamp-collecting-shop owner who quietly pocketed valuable stamps left behind by a client.

To their credit, the students also recognize integrity when they see it: The co-worker who found an envelope with $500 in cash and immediately turned it in; the woman who stopped her car, jumped a fence and ran through a pack of dogs to resuscitate a drowning toddler; the store manager who had the courage to fire her best friend and top salesperson because she was skimming the cash register.

They understand, as do all of us that doing the right thing can be painful, but it's still worth doing. Some of their examples are very personal.

Integrity is doing the right thing even when it hurts

One student wrote: "It takes a man of integrity to do what is right for his family rather than what is expedient and easy for himself. One example is my father. My dad was dealing with some tough realities about eight years ago. My mother had an extra-marital affair with another man while she lived in California for a nursing job. She became pregnant and had a baby boy. The easy thing for Dad to do would have been to divorce my mother and try to win custody of my brother and me. Instead, my father decided to do something many people probably couldn't handle; he made up his mind to keep the family together and try to work on forgiving my mother for her transgression.

"My father took in the baby and slowly accepted him as his own offspring. He did what he is best at, which is being a loving and accepting father. My father took excellent care of my brother and me as well. Dad had also started to reconnect and gain a loving relationship with Mom before she died in a car accident. That doesn't change the fact that my dad had an incredible amount of integrity to keep the family together and functioning. Some people, I think, could take my father's example and do what is best for other people, not just for themselves."

Think of how tough it must have been for that student's father to lay his ego aside, forgive all that had gone on and to, instead, work at rebuilding a family.

America was built to greatness by people who understood success wasn't about wealth or prestige. They knew real success comes from living to a higher standard. The world envies us for our wealth, but they admire us for our character. The very best of America is based on compassion, freedom, honesty, resourcefulness and a fierce determination to protect what is right.

In 2008, our national greed made our economy stumble and we took many of our global trading partners with us. But in the difficult times that followed there were lessons to be learned. The same lessons our parents learned from the Great Depression and World War.

We will all face hard times. That's not the point. The point is how we respond. We can give in to despair and quit or we can endure, repair and rebuild. In the process, each of us has the opportunity to discover what the people profiled here obviously knew; that a life built on integrity is the only one really worth living.

Questions for discussion:

- When have you shown integrity in a tough situation? How did it make you feel?
- One of our most lasting icons is the American Cowboy. For a light-hearted approach to the topic, go to the Vaquero Enterprises web site and look up The Cowboy Code (www. elvaquero.com/The_Cowboy_Code.htm). There you can see the "codes" of famous old-time radio and television cowboys from Gene Autry to Roy Rogers. While sure to make you smile, see if there aren't some things you might apply to your life.

For more on integrity:

- Watch the 1962 film "To Kill a Mockingbird" or read the original novel by Harper Lee. See how one man brings integrity to race-related tragedy.
- One of our most controversial presidents was Harry Truman. Do an Internet search on him and decide if you think he modeled integrity.

CONCLUSION

"Everyone needs to stop letting our materialistic society think
for them and realize that they have the power
to define success for themselves."
—Ryan Radford. (Age 18)

Now you have them. Twelve values that will help you redefine success and apply it to your life, a success based on not just following the example of others, but also the direction of your own moral compass.

We are confident in your ability to follow that compass to a better, more grounded, happier life. In the first chapter of this book, we wrote about the need to redefine success. Too often, we think of it as the acquisition of material possessions. But materialism is a mask that hides underlying problems. And our generation, the Baby Boom generation that came from those who persevered through the Great Depression and brought America through World War II, has unfortunately perpetuated this emphasis on material wealth, real or imagined.

In our effort to redefine success, we found surprising wisdom from the children of the current generation, the Millenials, who are often criticized for being lazy, demanding and having an inflated sense of entitlement. We've found otherwise. Here are some thoughts on success and life from a group of 20-something college students that speak to the heart of what we've tried to convey:

On Perseverance

"Sometimes success can also be measured by how you fail the challenges you are given." Dallas Kempton (Age 20).

On Laughter and Humor

"I have learned that money and nice things do not buy happiness, but being broke and living in your parents' basement doesn't work either." Matt Gypin (Age 27)

On Community

"Success is going to bed at night knowing that you gave to society in some way during the day." Matt Priesmeyer (Age 18)

On Love

"If you can live a life of love and respect towards your environment (people and the earth itself), I think you can call it a success." Eva Jirjahlke (Age 20)

On Faith

"If I have served God in my little corner of the world, I will have had a successful life." Shea Sikkema (Age 20)

On Integrity

"Success is being able to look yourself in the mirror every day without cringing." Lauren Gould (Age 20)

And Finally

"If you do the right thing, success will follow close behind." Keegan Jenks (Age 19)

EPILOGUE

"Celebrate! Celebrate! Celebrate!"
—Lynn Jefferson Elsberry

In the end, the decline came rapidly. In November he had hosted pheasant hunters from far-flung places. Two flew their own planes to Marshalltown just to walk Iowa fields and enjoy the hospitality of his tidy two-bedroom apartment. He welcomed the scruffy looking crew of adopted sons with hearty home-cooked meals of pork chops and pot roasts. He'd share a glass of red wine and could still bring the house down with a well-placed wisecrack.

Just a few days after we left from an early Christmas celebration, he called to say it was time. Time to move to the care facility where he had been volunteering for so many years. The administrator came in on Christmas Eve to personally welcome him to his second home. Seven people, residents and staff, stopped to say the same thing as he went to dinner the first night.

Not for him the loneliness of old age. A constant stream of visitors came and went from his room. Staff members would come in on their day off to help him go to a doctor's appointment. Notes, cards and phone calls filled the rest of his days. Ninety-four years of giving to others continued to pay him dividends until the very end.

He never lost his optimism or ability to joke, but his unfailing energy finally began to seep away. Near the end, he spent more and more time sleeping only to awaken with a weary smile when visitors showed up.

As we talked one Friday in May, he agreed to go to the doctor's appointment we'd set up for him. Mostly I think he did it for us. When he declined the appointment earlier that day, he told the nurse there was a time and place for everything. Dad didn't want to spend the phone call talking about doctors; he wanted to talk about other things. He was fighting for air, and it was tough for him to speak, but this is what he said.

"Don't worry about me, boys. I'm ready. God has touched me. He's touched me, and I'm ready to go see your mother—the most wonderful woman who ever lived. I've missed her and so many others; we had so many good friends. I'm ready to go see them all."

"Don't worry about me. When the time comes I want you to celebrate! Celebrate! Celebrate our family and your mother and our good times. No man ever had two better sons, and no two men ever had better wives. I'm so very proud of you all. So was your mother. You've been so good to me. I can never thank you enough."

Still a great planner and quipster to the end he said, "Have a big old bash at the church. I stopped giving them money a while back and maybe that will square my account with them!"

Laughing now through my tears I listened as he said, "There's not much we haven't said to each other, but I do want you to know God has touched me and I'm ready to go. I guess I've waited my whole life to say that. I love you, love you, love you very much. Goodbye."

Later that evening, he told his nurse to give him a good shower because he was ready to go. She did just that and tucked him into bed.

That night, amid the drone and beep of the monitors and the soft murmur from the corridors, he slipped away to see the farm girl with a smile that could always melt his heart.

The funeral was the celebration he asked for. Set in the church of both his youth and old age, the crowd of family and friends sang his favorite hymns and told stories and jokes. We laughed and we cried and we rejoiced in a life well lived. We had the "big old bash" in the church basement as directed, and it was a time of more laughter and memories, just as he would have wanted.

Later on with the crowds gone and ties loosened, a good friend from out of state settled into an easy chair and began to talk. Having only met our father a few times, he spoke at some length about all he'd heard that day.

He summed up like this, "You know," he said thoughtfully, "your father just taught you how to die." And then after a bit more consideration he added, "But more importantly, he taught you how to live."

NOTES

CHAPTER 1

[1] McCullough, David. Undergraduate Ceremony Address, University of Connecticut, May 15, 1999. *www.commencement.uconn.edu/history/ . . . /1999_**McCullough**.php*

CHAPTER 3

[1] Covey, Stephen, 7 Habits of Highly Effective People (Singapore: Franklin Covey Co., 1998), 35.

[2] McGinnis, Alan Loy, The Power of Optimism, (San Francisco: Harper and Row, 1990), 3.

[3] Robinson, Bryan E., Chained to the Desk (New York: New York University Press, 2007) 15.

[4] Davis, Martha; Eshelman, Elizabeth; McKay, Mathew; The Relaxation and Stress Reduction Workbook (Oakland: New Harbinger Publications, 1982), 91.

CHAPTER 4

[1] Expansion Multiples of GDP for 15 Economies, 1950-1999 (Ratio of GDP in 1999 to GDP in 1950, international dollars), Maddison,

2001; World Bank, World Development Indicators Online (http://www. worldbank.org/data/wdi2004/index.htm).

[2] Zaslow, Jeffrey, "The Entitlement Epidemic: Who's Really to Blame?" Wall Street Journal, July 19, 2007.

CHAPTER 6

[1] Smith, Marti, "Serious Thoughts About Humor," Telling Secrets blog, January 12, 2009, http://tellingsecretsmks.blogspot.com/2009_01_01_archive.html

[2] Cousins, Norman, Anatomy of an Illness (New York and London: W.W. Norton & Co., 1979), page 44.

[3] University of Maryland Medical Center, "Volunteers were shown funny and disturbing movies to test the effect of emotions on blood vessels," news release, http://www.umm.edu/news/releases/laughter2.htm.

[4] Godsey, Kim, "Americans Can Achieve Financial Peace" Greeley Tribune, September 9, 2008.

[5] Boardman, Calvin and Sandomir, Alan, Foundations of Business Thought, 7th Edition, "The Dependence Affect from the Affluent Society" by Galbraith, John (Boston, MA: Pearson Custom Publishing) 304.

CHAPTER 7

[1] Putnam, Robert D., Bowling Alone (New York: Simon & Schuster, New York, 2000) 326.

[2] England, Dan, "Lives Rebuilt: Couple Reclaims Lives with Help," Greeley Tribune, January 1, 2009.

[3] Bernuth, Katharine, "Working Through the Pain," Panorama, published by Greeley Tribune, 2006.

[4] England, Dan, "A Knowing Smile," Panorama, published by Greeley Tribune, 2006.

CHAPTER 8

1 Collins, Jim, Good to Great (New York: Harper Business, 2001) 21.
2 Peters, Mike, "Family Recalls Woman's Passions," Greeley Tribune, September 25, 2007.

CHAPTER 9

1 Ornish, Dean, Love and Survival (New York: HarperCollins, 1998).
2 Scarborough, Lynn Wilford, Talk Like Jesus (Beverly Hills, CA: Phoenix Books, 2007), page 56.
3 Dunn, David, Try Giving Yourself Away (New York: Prentice Hall Press, 1970).

CHAPTER 10

1 Kovacs, Joe, "Colts Coach More Proud of Christ than 'Blackness,'" WorldNetDaily.com, February 4, 2007, http://www.wnd.com/news/article.asp?ARTICLE_ID=54098.
2 Gibson, Lisa, Life in Death: Journey from Terrorism to Triumph (Xulon Press, 2008) 145-146.
3 Gibson, 187-188.
4 Gibson, 203.

CHAPTER 11

1 Delgado, Vanessa, "We're Legal, Family Says," Greeley Tribune, October 20, 2006.
2 Hymowitz, Carol, "In the Lead," Wall Street Journal, January 29, 2007.
3 Miller, Stephen, "Mad in the U.S.A.," Wall Street Journal, December 30, 2006.

CHAPTER I2

[1] Imprimis, Volume 20, Number 9.
[2] Wilstein, Steve, "A Football Coach Does the 'Right Thing,'" Associated Press, November 24, 2002.
[3] "Hayes Turns Himself in for Using Wrong Ball" ESPN.com, November 19, 2008, http://sports.espn.go.com/golf/news/story?id=3712372.

Made in the USA
Lexington, KY
07 January 2013